Hot Cho

With

Devot

Hot Chocolate
With God
Devotional

Real Questions & Answers
from Girls Just Like You

Camryn Kelly

with Jill and Erin Kelly

New York Boston Nashville

All Scripture quotations, unless otherwise indicated, are taken from THE HOLY BIBLE, NEW INTERNATIONAL VERSION®. NIV®. Copyright © 1973, 1978, 1984 by Biblica, Inc™. Used by permission of Zondervan. All rights reserved.

Scripture quotations marked NKJV are taken from the New King James Version®. Copyright © 1982 by Thomas Nelson, Inc. Used by permission. All rights reserved.

Scripture quotations marked *The Message* are taken from *The Message*. Copyright © 1993, 1994, 1995, 1996, 2000, 2001, 2002 by NavPress Publishing Group. Used by permission. All rights reserved.

FaithWords
Hachette Book Group
237 Park Avenue
New York, NY 10017

www.faithwords.com

Printed in the United States of America

WOR

First Edition: October 2013

10 9 8 7 6 5 4 3 2 1

FaithWords is a division of Hachette Book Group, Inc.
The FaithWords name and logo are trademarks of Hachette Book Group, Inc.

The Hachette Speakers Bureau provides a wide range of authors for speaking events. To find out more, go to www.hachettespeakersbureau.com or call (866) 376-6591.

The publisher is not responsible for websites (or their content) that are not owned by the publisher.

Library of Congress Control Number: 2013941574
ISBN: 978-1-4555-2856-1

This very SWEET DEVO is
dedicated to all the amazing,
incredible, CHOSEN-BY-GOD
GIRLS, who shared their
hopes, fears, doubts, dreams,
and questions with us!
We LOVE you!
YOU ROCK!

This Super-Sweet Devo belongs to:

Avery McGee

Don't let anyone look down on you because you are young, but set an example for the believers in speech, in life, in love, in faith and in purity.

1 Timothy 4:12

Thank you...

All the Girls—This devotional would not have been possible without all the cool questions we received from YOU—the girls who took the time to share their hearts and hurts with us. We're so thankful for you, and we love you. Oh, and we're praying for you!

Rick Kern—We thank God for you and for your friendship and for always being there to help us make everything *Hot Chocolate With God*—shine for Jesus.

The FaithWords team—Jana, you're great, and we love you and Kenzie. Thank you for everything!

Team Wolgemuth—Thank you for loving us and for helping us make HCWG a reality. We are so grateful for all of you.

To my mom and sister, Erin—It's devo time! I just love that God has blessed us with each other. I don't know what I would do without you. I LOVE YOU SO MUCH!

Finally, to Jesus—Thank You for creating everything HCWG! YOU ARE AMAZING! Thank You for loving me and for helping me and the girls that read this book to keep YOU as our first LOVE! Please help us to live for YOU and LOVE You more each and every day!

Contents

This is NOT a typical devotional...

Seriously, nothing about *Hot Chocolate With God* has ever been or will ever be typical.

What I mean by this is that everything you're going to experience here is epically (not sure if that is even a word) great and beyond what you've experienced so far in any other devotional-type books.

Whoa, I don't even like calling this a book. Even though it looks and feels like a book, the *HCWG Devotional* is MORE than just another book, which is why it's so NOT typical.

Why?

Well, because you're not just a typical girl.

You're God's girl—and that makes you more than ordinary. More than extraordinary!

Come on, we absolutely must try to get our hearts wrapped around this important fact before we go any farther:

9

YOU ARE GOD'S IDEA, WONDERFULLY AND FEARFULLY MADE ON PURPOSE— FOR A PURPOSE.

So everything about you matters—to God...and to me. ☺

This book is made up of all (at least as much as we were able to fit—because, believe me, this book could've been five times the size that it is if we would've included everything) that matters—everything that MATTERS to you, RIGHT NOW, in your journey called LIFE—in this moment.

It's more than a devotional. It's not at all typical.

It's *you*! Your questions. Your life.

Which is why there's nothing typical about what you'll experience as you continue to read on. Besides, you're hanging out with me, and certainly, if you know me at all—even a little bit—you know that I can be a little bit ridiculous and epic, ha-ha-ha! I figured I already said the word "typical" way too many times, so I decided to say "epic" instead.

Whatever!

So here's the deal. A lot of cool things have happened since we published the *Hot Chocolate With God* book series and set up the *HCWG* website (www .hotchocolatewithgod.com). One of the greatest blessings is that my sister, Erin, and I have been asked to come and speak to girls about all things *HCWG*. (Um, and it's kind of scary to speak in front of people, yeah.) Well, as a result of talking to so many girls about so many things, we have received hundreds of really honest and important questions from girls.

That's what's in this book—QUESTIONS about anything and everything that seems to matter to girls like you and me.

But let me just tell you something—**WE DON'T HAVE IT ALL FIGURED OUT!**

Erin and I read through all the questions (with my mother and grammie, it was so cool, and we prayed for the girls too! And yes, I'm getting sidetracked, oops— what can I say, it's a gift. LOL!).

After reading your questions, we decided to share how we would answer the questions; therefore, when you see "Cam," you'll know that it's my answer to the question. When you see "Erin," my sister is sharing her answer. Yes, she's four years older than I am, and she really is blessed with wisdom. I love her, and I think you will too when you get to know her more through what she shares here.

Okay, so we share our answers—**BUT**…

BUT…

GOD shares His too!

What?

Yes, God has an answer for every single question you have! (P.S. In this book and as far as God is concerned, there are no stupid questions—just thought I'd let you know. ☺)

But remember (and yes, I know this is hard to do), God holds the answers to **ALL** of our questions, but sometimes He chooses not to tell us. In other words, He wants us to trust Him, trust that He knows even though He chooses not to let us know. I read once that life is about the journey, not so much about getting to the destination. Well, sometimes what's best for us is seeking after the heart of the One who has the answer rather than getting the answer. Do you get it? God knows best, and teaching us to trust might just be what He is building in our hearts when the answers don't come or aren't what we hoped for.

I'm sorry if what I just said is confusing—sometimes I'm all over the place in my mind and it comes out in my writing...yikes!

Anyway, this is what we need to remember and never forget:

GOD HAS GIVEN US EVERYTHING WE NEED FOR LIFE!

Including **ANSWERS** to some of our questions.

We find what He wants us to know in His Word—the Bible.

So not only do we share how we would respond to these questions, we also share God's response found in His Word.

In fact, let's just make this super clear: **HIS ANSWER** is the only one that actually matters, because His Word is the final word!

Erin and I love sharing with you, but ultimately God is God and He's perfect, so what He has to say is all we really need to know!

Got me on this?

Are you with me?

If you know me, you know that I'm with you. I'll be praying every step of the way.

Sooo…

Let's go!

Oh, and by the way…

You. Are. Great.

Believe it, girlfriend! And just in case you didn't hear me the first time…

YOU! ARE! GREAT!

Love you,
Camryn ("Cam")

What you need to know...

Clearly there are some things you need to know, and I'm here to fill you in. If you're already familiar with the way we do things in the *HCWG* world—SWEET! If this is your first opportunity to hang out with us, KEEP READING!

1. **PRIVACY POLICY!** What you say here—stays here. This is a safe place to share how you feel and say what you want. A place to be YOU! So fear not—be real and share your heart!

2. Website action! YES! Throughout this sweet, not-so-typical devo I will ask you to go to the *Hot Chocolate With God* website (www.hotchocolatewithgod.com) to view **Cam Clips**. When you see a **Cam Clip**, there will be a special code word next to it. Then at the **Cam Clips** section of the website you will type in these special codes to view the fun videos. No one can view these videos without typing in the code exactly as you see it in the book.

3. **IMPORTANT! DO NOT FORGET** to ask your parents before you get on the Internet. There's a lot of junk out there, and it's super important to protect your

eyes and ears from what can harm your heart. So MAKE SURE you ask your parents!

4. During your *Hot Chocolate With God Devotional* experience, you will read **Sweet Truths**. These *are awesome*, incredible words from God's book—the Bible. If you've never read the Bible, that's totally okay. God reveals His heart and talks to us through His Word. And remember what I already said: What God has to say really is all that matters!

5. Lastly, *you* rock! Yeah, you do! I'm so excited to see what God will do as you share this time with Him. Before you go, I just want to tell you that you will get out of this what you put into it. I just had a great idea. Maybe before you read each devo question you can say a quick prayer, something like this: "Lord, please help me to know You more." Or maybe just ask Him to help you understand better what He wants to teach you as you read through each devotion. Whatever you decide will be great! Have fun!

Sweet Section

1

Fashion, frustrations, fears, beauty, and body—the inside and outside of it all

What do you do if you're unsure of yourself?
—*Jackie*

Cam: If we were hanging out together right now, the first thing I would ask you is this: *Why are you unsure about yourself? Are you comparing yourself to other girls? Did your friends or someone say something to you to make you feel unsure about who you are?* I would ask you these questions so I might be able to better help you. I don't really know what else to say except that **God KNOWS you and He LOVES you**. Whatever you need to know in order to feel secure and loved you can find in Him!

And don't forget that being unsure is also part of growing up. Like most girls, Erin and I are constantly facing new experiences, and I'm not always Miss Confident, if ya know what I mean. Seriously, I struggle and I'm unsure of myself a lot. I read somewhere that experience is the best teacher, and these new experiences do just that: teach me if I let them.

Like I said, sometimes meeting new people or doing new things makes me nervous and unsure. But I have to ask myself: Will I overcome the situation, or will I let the situation overcome me? And that's when I have to remember what the Bible says in Romans 8:37, "No, in all these things we are more than conquerors through him who loved us." I might feel like the situation is bigger than I am, but I know God is bigger than the situation—and through Him, I can overcome it.

Erin: You may be unsure of yourself. You may have doubts about who you are. But God *knows* who you are. He knows everything about you, and He loves you just the way you are. Seek God and His heart so you can be sure of who He is and who you are in Him. Jesus is absolutely sure about you!

You were created by God—for God!

To find out more about who you are and what God thinks of you, **READ THE BIBLE**! Camryn and I will tell you this at least a hundred times. If you've never read the Bible before, don't worry about it. Today is a great day to start reading! I would suggest you start in the New Testament, beginning with the Gospel of John. If you need help, let us know or ask someone that you know who reads the Bible. If you don't know anyone, just ask **GOD** to help you. Before you seek God through His Word, **PRAY** and ask Him to show you who HE is and who you are.

Sweet Truth

This is how we know that we belong to the truth and how we set our hearts at rest in his presence: If our hearts condemn us, we know that God is greater than our hearts, and he knows everything. —1 John 3:19-20

Just Cool

Have you ever played cards? What's your favorite game? I like a lot of card games. In some games, the dealer names a *wild card,* which can be anything and it's more valuable than the other cards. It always amazes me when someone names a joker as the wild card because then that little joker (*the least valuable, weakest card in the deck that doesn't even have a number on it*) can actually have the same value as an ace (*the most valuable, strongest card in the deck*). So if someone lays down kings and you lay down jokers, your jokers overcome the kings!

Well, as crazy as it sounds (you know me, girl—I can be crazy with a capital "C"), in many ways the Father, Son, and Holy Spirit are like our wild cards in the game of life. God has given us—His children—His power over situations; over the hand we're dealt in life, even when circumstances go against us. I heard about this man who used to carry a joker in his wallet to remind him that whatever cards life dealt him, he could always play the wild cards that God gave him. Maybe you want to carry a joker as a reminder in your purse or backpack too! Try it!

What should I do if I feel discouraged and let down? —*Anne*

Cam: Go to God, girl! He's always there for you when you're struggling and discouraged about anything and everything. And it may help to know that you're in really good company. Lots of people in the Bible struggled with discouragement. Like King David. He was a man after God's own heart (1 Samuel 13:14), and he was a real king—yes, the kind that wear big crowns and rule over people. He went through a lot but hung on to God for dear life!

In Psalm 42:5, David cried out, "Why, my soul,

are you downcast? Why so disturbed within me? Put your hope in God, for I will yet praise him, my Savior and my God." Downcast means discouraged, or really super bummed out. Even Jesus struggled with those kinds of feelings. Hebrews 5:7 says that Jesus Himself "offered up prayers and supplications with strong crying and tears..." (KJV).

So if Bible people had to deal with feelings of discouragement, we can all expect to find ourselves in the same sort of battle now and then, right? When I feel discouraged, sad, and totally bummed out, the first person I usually go to is my mom. She's always there for me and tries to help me understand what God would want me to do. If you don't feel like you can go to your mom and dad, or a special adult in your life that you trust, God is always there for you, no matter what. Just talk to Him.

Tell Him what's on your heart.

Talk to Him about what's bothering you. He knows every detail about everything and He wants to help you. Just because you don't see Him doesn't mean He's not there—He's with you even now!

Erin: Everyone has moments when they feel discouraged or let down. Whether it's by parents, siblings, friends, classmates—whoever. There will be moments when people will tell you, "You can't." At times like this, you have an opportunity to show people and yourself that with Jesus "you can." In Christ and through His strength you can do all things. Things you never ever dreamed you could do.

If you find that your friends are always discouraging you, pray for them and ask God to help you be an encouragement to them. I know this sounds crazy and really hard—right? Like, why would you want to encourage and pray for someone who is always discouraging you and bringing you down? Well, of course you have a choice as far as how you would respond. We all have a choice. I've found that even if someone is mean to me, if I repay him or her with God's love and kindness, it keeps anger and frustration from filling my mind and heart.

Ultimately, only God can encourage you in the way you need it most. Don't let others bring you down. If you belong to the Lord, then trust Him with all that concerns you today.

For the LORD himself goes before you and will be with you; he will never leave you nor forsake you. Do not be afraid; do not be discouraged. —Deuteronomy 31:8

Just Cool

Hey, we have an idea! Go get a 3×5-inch card. If you don't have one just grab a half sheet of lined paper or whatever. Got it? Great! Now, write the verse above on your card and then decorate it. Get creative, girl! You can do it! When you're done, tape your reminder card in a place where you will read it every single day. Lastly, READ and BELIEVE! P.S. God is for you! Oh, and we love you. ☺

Why do girls always feel like they have to look perfect? I hear my friends complain that they are ugly or fat. I don't know how to convince them that they are

beautiful and being perfect is overrated. God made us the way we are. Help? *—Jamie*

Cam: Oh my goodness, so many girls have asked us this sort of question through our website. It's obviously a huge, annoying problem. I hear you loud and clear, yet I almost don't even know where to begin.

Proverbs 23:7 says, "For as he thinks within himself, so he is." (Oh, that's the NASV translation BTW, which I usually don't use—but it really helps to explain this better.) Anyhow, I'm not a walking Bible girl, but I want so badly for us to understand how to deal with these sorts of things.

Hey, when you watch TV, have you noticed how incredibly ridiculous some of the commercials are? I mean, wow, think about it!

○ Your hair is dull and boring—you need our shampoo.

○ Your armpits totally stink—get our deodorant before all the boys notice.

○ Your teeth are an icky shade of green—you gotta get our whitening toothpaste!

I could go on and on! Ugh! And what about all the alcohol commercials? Are you serious? It's like all the pretty girls drink beer, and the boys like them because of the beer they drink. RIDICULOUS!

Why wouldn't we feel like we're not good enough when most TV advertisements and magazines tell us that we need so much more to be "cool"? Argh, I'm getting frustrated, can you tell?

Erin: I agree with Cam. That message is totally reinforced everywhere you turn. The other thing is that you can't convince your friends they're beautiful; it's something they have to believe for themselves. And as long as they compare themselves with the superficial things that this world says are meaningful, they'll continue to believe the ugly lie that they're not good enough!

I mean, true beauty is an inner thing, right? Just check out the **Sweet Truth**.

It's not that God is down on us for trying to look our best. What I think He's saying is that true beauty is *who* you are more than what you look like. I know you want to convince your friends that they're beautiful, but that can be kind of scary. *If you can convince them that they are beautiful, then couldn't someone else convince them that they aren't?* On the other hand, if they see that your beauty shines from within as a reflection of Christ living in you, not based on outward appearance—then maybe they won't be obsessed with trying to look perfect. The way I look at it: If you're good enough for Jesus, you're good enough for me—and that covers everyone!

Your beauty should not come from outward adornment, such as elaborate hairstyles and the wearing of gold jewelry or fine clothes. Rather, it should be that of your inner self, the unfading beauty of a gentle and quiet spirit, which is of great worth in God's sight.
—1 Peter 3:3-4

I don't have enough money to buy the latest fashions. I get made fun of because I don't have what all the other girls have. What am I supposed to do about this? *—Anita*

Cam: I'm sorry that there is some sort of style issue according to your peers, and I get really frustrated about the focus on fashion these days. To have others make fun of you because you don't dress in the latest styles just makes me sad. *What matters is who we are (like that we are His ☺)— not what we appear to be*, if you get me. I'd rather hang with a true friend in faded fashion than some mean glamour girl in the best styles.

We need to love and pray for Ms. Glamour Girl and all those who are making fun of you. It's really hard, but these girls need Jesus, and if you don't pray for them— who will? If you don't care enough to try and love them, then who will? Ask God to give you HIS love for them.

These girls know that what they're doing is wrong; they know they wouldn't want to be treated like they are treating you. God will give you what you need in order to deal with this. I'll be praying for you. Stay tough in Jesus!

Erin: I almost don't know where to start, but how about Jesus' attitude toward money and fashion? Jesus actually shared a message in the Gospel of Matthew called the "Sermon on the Mount," and it's really cool because believe it or not, in that message He actually talks about your question.

Here's part of it, "And why do you worry about clothes? See how the lilies of the field grow. They do not labor or spin. Yet

I tell you that not even Solomon in all his splendor was dressed like one of these. If that is how God clothes the grass of the field, which is here today and tomorrow is thrown into the fire, will he not much more clothe you, O you of little faith? So do not worry, saying, 'What shall we eat?' or 'What shall we drink?' or 'What shall we wear?' For the pagans run after all these things, and your heavenly Father knows that you need them. But seek first his kingdom and his righteousness, and all these things will be given to you as well." (Matthew 6:28–33)

I don't think you need to be a faith queen to get what God is saying here. It's pretty clear what our attitude toward clothes and fashion should be: what God's attitude is. Jesus is saying trust God, He knows what you need and will hook you up. Don't waste your energy sweating over what you need to get by in this world. So many people waste their lives doing this. Instead Jesus tells us to seek the kingdom of God first and foremost and He'll be sure we have everything we need. It's almost like He's saying, "You take care of my kingdom, and I'll take care of yours."

So...I guess when all is said and done, God loves these girls and He wants to love them through you. He's asking you to trust Him with everything. To seek His kingdom in your life instead of wishing for a closet full of fashion. Hang on to this awesome promise in Philippians 4:19, "And my God will meet all your needs according to the riches of his glory in Christ Jesus."

Therefore I tell you, do not worry about your life, what you will eat or drink; or about your body, what you will wear. Is not life more important than food, and the body more important than clothes? —Matthew 6:25

THIS IS GOING TO BE SUPPA COOL! Okay, did you just hear me shout that last sentence at the top of my lungs? Ha-ha-ha! We think this is a great way to remember what we've just talked about. We'll call this *Rockin' the Prayer Closet*—an epic devo with the Kelly girls.

It might be easier to actually show you

rather than give you a bunch of instructions for this one. YES—it's a **Cam Clip** moment! We've been waiting to get one of these in here.

CAM CLIPS CODE: ROCKIN THE PRAYER CLOSET

I get frustrated very easily. Any ideas on how to stay calm? —*Kinsey*

Cam: Unfortunately, this is something I deal with too. Sometimes I get frustrated really easily. It pretty much all depends on things like my mood, the amount of sleep I've had, circumstances, and more. What I do know is that when I gave my heart to Jesus I was made new, and the Bible explains that the fruit of the Spirit is growing in me. (That sounds so weird—fruit growing in me. Like, do I have bananas and grapes growing in my belly? Ha-ha-ha!)

Galatians 5:22–23 says, "But the fruit of the Spirit is love, joy, peace, patience, kindness, goodness, faithfulness, gentleness, self-control." This "fruit" helps with frustration, especially the joy, peace, patience, and self-control part. Ya know, we are always learning. You need to be encouraged right now because God isn't finished with you yet. He will help you with both the things that frustrate you and your attitude toward them.

Erin: There are a lot of Bible verses that talk about peace, and when I think of being frustrated, it seems to me that what I really need to do is focus on the peace of God. For this one, I'm just going to share a few powerful promises about the peace of God that we can believe for ourselves. I encourage you to read these and really think about what God is saying to you, my friend.

> "For God is not a God of disorder but of peace."
> —1 Corinthians 14:33

> "And the peace of God, which transcends all understanding, will guard your hearts and your minds in Christ Jesus." —Philippians 4:7

> "Now may the Lord of peace himself give you peace at all times and in every way. The Lord be with all of you." —2 Thessalonians 3:16

Think about some of these truths in relationship to the frustration you struggle with. The Lord is the Lord of peace and can give you peace at all times, in every way—including when you're frustrated. Furthermore, we are told that the peace of God will guard your heart and mind—that means against (among other things) frustration. I could go on and on, sister, but I think you're getting it. So PEACE OUT!

Let the peace of Christ rule in your hearts, since as members of one body you were called to peace. And be thankful.
—Colossians 3:15

I went through a really bad experience that I'm having a hard time forgetting. How can I deal with this hurt always coming into my mind?
—GirlNeedsHelp

Cam: Hey, girl! I'm so glad you shared and opened your heart up to us about this horrible hurt. I think I can sort of relate to what you're talking about because I went through a really bad experience too—the death of my eight-year-old brother whom I absolutely loved. I can tell you, there are no easy answers to hard questions, and what you're dealing with seems pretty hard.

God is the only One big enough to deal with this. And He is so compassionate—I really love Psalm 34:17–19, "The righteous cry out, and the LORD hears them; he delivers them from all their troubles. The LORD is close to the brokenhearted and saves those who are crushed in spirit. The righteous person may have many troubles, but the LORD delivers him from them all." Seek God, my friend. It might be hard to believe, but He really is close to the broken-hearted, and He'll help you.

Erin: I hear the cry of your heart; my mother, grammie, sister, and I were all "GirlsNeedHelp" for quite a while after my brother, Hunter, went to heaven. And though it takes time, I can promise from experience that no matter how deep the pain is, God's healing love is deeper.

There are a couple things that have helped me along the way; maybe they'll help you too. First, you said that you are having a hard time forgetting about this experience and I think that's because sometimes we just can't! Some things we go through in life are so hurtful that they change us, and in that way they're always with us. So let me encourage you to stop trying to forget, but instead remember that whatever it is, God is with you to help you every step of the way.

The other thing is that if someone else was involved in whatever this bad experience was, it's really important to forgive them. Unforgiveness seems to make us continue to remember the hurt. We need God's forgiveness, and He is ready and willing to help us. In my own way I had to forgive the Lord for taking Hunter, but He helped me and gave me the power to accept, forgive, and heal. I'll be praying for you, and I hope you stay in touch and let us know how you're doing.

And we know that in all things God works for the good of those who love him, who have been called according to his purpose. —Romans 8:28

What do you do about the fear of new situations, like going to a new school and not knowing anyone? —*Sunny*

Cam: New situations can be scary; many times you just don't know what to expect. I think the answer for how to deal with this is all in our attitude. If we look at a new experience like changing schools, with a bad attitude, we're already bummed out before we attend our first class. However, if we go into a new situation trusting and believing that God is in control—we're already heading in the right direction. God's with you, He's not going to let you down, and He always has a blessing for you in the midst of whatever changes He allows into your life.

Erin: When we don't know what's waiting for us it can be really intimidating, but I try to approach new situations with faith, believing that God is already there waiting for me. When I do that, I don't rely on my own strength. Instead, I conquer my fear with faith. It helps to sort of take the initiative to make friends or do what I'm there to do.

I also trust that God sent me into the new situation for a reason. Think about Abraham, whom the Lord called to leave his home without even telling him where he was going—can you even imagine? "The LORD had said to Abram, 'Go from your country, your people and your father's household to the land I will show you'" (Genesis 12:1). That had to be really scary—but God gave him the strength to go for it as he moved forward in faith. I get scared too; I think that's normal. The real issue is not letting your fear overcome your faith, but overcoming fear with faith. AMEN!

Sweet Truth

The LORD is my light and my salvation—whom shall I fear? The LORD is the stronghold of my life—of whom shall I be afraid?
—Psalm 27:1

Journal It

We are big on journaling in the Kelly family. Well, my daddy isn't and our three dogs don't journal either—at least I don't think they do. Ridiculous! I know! ☺ Anyway, we think it's time for some serious journaling. We've provided this very cool, HGWG-girl-style piece of journal paper for you. Notice it has been "Camified" (I created a new word)—the candy—yay!

Start by talking to God about everything you're afraid of right now. Let it all out. Ask Him to help you overcome all of these things—and be specific. Okay?

People call me ugly, and I think I'm ugly. What should I do? —*Awbrey*

Cam: (Warning: This will be the longest devotion you'll probably ever read. But it's important—so **KEEP READING**!) Okay, first of all you're NOT ugly. That's just a total lie. Who told you that you were ugly? It certainly wasn't God, I mean, consider the source. Of course, no one is perfect but God, and He made you, and He never makes mistakes.

What you look like is how God chose to make you, and He does everything good and right, exactly how it should be. You are you! Instead of wishing you looked prettier or different maybe, you can ask God to help you to be thankful for how He made you. At the very least, we all should be thankful just to be alive. Don't listen to these mean people—ask God to help them.

It's not easy, but I have found that praying for people who hurt me brings me closer to Jesus. And it's pretty clear that these people you're referring to *really* need prayer.

And another thing, sometimes girls compare themselves to magazine models and people on television. It's ridiculous but we all do it, and when we do, we're usually very disappointed. My mom has read articles about these models being made to look prettier than they really are by being "airbrushed" to hide their flaws. I don't even own an airbrush, but if I did I wouldn't try to impress other people by changing photos of myself with it! Don't compare yourself with these cover girls because God loves you for who you are.

And get this: The Bible says that Jesus wasn't very handsome at all. Check this out, it's talking about Jesus' appearance. The Bible says: "He had no beauty or majesty to attract us to him, nothing in his appearance that we should desire him" (Isaiah 53:2b). What drew people to Jesus was His heart and the way He loved and lived—not how cool or good-looking He was.

Jesus didn't want to be a rock star, and I guarantee He wasn't trying to trade in His robe for leather pants or the Bible for a cover story on *People* magazine (with an airbrushed photo, ha-ha-ha). He wouldn't want you to have a poster of Him on your wall or have you ask for His autograph. Can you imagine THAT—getting Jesus' autograph? I can see it now—I'd ask Him to sign my Bible, and He'd write in bright-blue Sharpie:

To Cam:

Thanks for reading My Word. Keep walking by faith, young princess warrior.

Best wishes and many blessings!

Your Lord,

Jesus

I don't mean any disrespect, I truly love God—but you can see how silly and weird it seems to the things that really matter when we put it like that.

In fact, Scripture says that instead of signing autographs, Jesus will write *our name* in the Lamb's Book of Life and acknowledge it before God the Father and all the angels (Revelation 3:5). Now *that's* really cool!

As far as those people who called you ugly, I don't think they would be very comfortable with the Bible right now because 1 Samuel 16:7 flat out says that people focus on looks, but God focuses on the heart (I put that in a **Sweet Truth** below ☺). He cares about you loving Him with all of your heart. Sooo, let's start focusing more on God and less on ourselves, more on His perfect love and less on our imperfections. Are you with me? COOL!

Erin: This really upsets me, and I wish I could hug you rather than just answer your question. People can be so mean! Here's the deal—God loves you! He made you exactly how He wanted you to be. We all look at other girls and think they are prettier than we are, but the truth is it doesn't matter, *you* are beautiful to God and that's **ALL** that matters.

You are beautiful—because you are the only you that He has created!

People hurt God when they say mean things to you about what you look like. He made you, and He never makes mistakes! There's an old saying, "Hurting people hurt people," and maybe some of these people are speaking out of their own sadness. Maybe these very people who have called you ugly have been called ugly by other people. Do you know what I mean? Or maybe they've been mistreated and hurt badly in other ways and now they're choosing to take out their own pain on you.

I don't really know for sure, but this is so sad. You might think I'm totally crazy for suggesting this, but maybe you should try to pray for these people—just like Cam said. That's in the Bible too; in Luke 6:28 Jesus said, "Bless those who curse you, pray for those who mistreat you." I know it may seem so hard, but if you ask God for the strength to do this He will honor such a beautiful desire.

One more thing. If we listen and take to heart the negative things people say, we will eventually start to believe them. Maybe that's why you think you're ugly. This makes me think of a very powerful **Sweet Truth**, so we will share two with you—the first one is the one I'm thinking of right now. We need to focus our minds on what is *true* and take our thoughts captive to what God says instead of what others say.

We demolish arguments and every pretension that sets itself up against the knowledge of God, and we take captive every thought and make it obedient to Christ.
—2 Corinthians 10:5

The LORD does not look at the things man looks at. Man looks at the outward appearance, but the LORD looks at the heart. —1 Samuel 16:7

Just Cool

We have a beyond brilliant idea! Get a piece of paper and write this on it: **God thinks I'm beautiful—therefore I am BEAUTIFUL.** Put this on a mirror that you look into every day! Read it! Believe it! Oh, and we're going to pray for you too! Our prayer is that when you look into the mirror, you see a beautiful girl made by an awesome, incredible GOD!

Sometimes I lie so people will think I'm cool. Like I pretend that I have money and things that I really don't. Can you help me? —Renee

Cam: I think it's really amazing that you're willing to talk about this—it takes a lot of courage. So right now I just need to tell you—YOU ROCK! It sounds like you're worried about what people think of you and feel like you're not good enough. As cool as this image you've created with all of your pretending seems to be, you're still pretending and it isn't real. It's got to be hard to live that way, never knowing if someone is going to catch you in a lie.

Maybe a good place to start is with the truth. You don't have to pretend because you're totally cool in God's eyes. He made you just the way you are, and He loves you—end of story! If you're willing to start being honest, God will bless you and help you move forward. He doesn't want you to pretend to be someone you're not, He loves YOU, not a version of yourself that's trying to impress others.

Erin: I'm amazed by your desire to change your life—way to go! I can't help but come back to Jeremiah 29:11, "'For I know the plans I have for you,' declares the LORD, 'plans to prosper you and not to harm you, plans to give you hope and a future.'" God has plans for YOU, not the person you pretend to be. He wants to prosper YOU and give YOU a hope and a future!

It might be hard to change old habits, but it's so worth it. You've got to believe what the Bible says about the plans God has for you, then follow Ephesians 4:25, "Therefore each of you must put off falsehood and speak truthfully to your neighbor, for we are all members of one body."

Start living honestly—God loves you for who you are, and He's the one who matters.

When you hide behind all kinds of lies you're just hurting yourself—and Him, because He made you to be who you are, not who you aren't. So start by believing in His love for YOU, and refuse to be anyone but who you are.

 **Instead, speaking the truth in love, we will grow to become in every respect the mature body of him who is the head, that is, Christ.** —Ephesians 4:15

How can I have more self-control? I know I shouldn't do certain things but I end up doing them anyway. —*katarina balarina*

Cam: I love this question. The fact that you want more self-control so you're able to stop doing things you know you shouldn't is totally cool. You're not alone in your struggle—I don't know anyone who doesn't wrestle with this, including yours truly. The one HUGE thing that comes to my mind is that self-control is a fruit of the Spirit. Remember, we already talked a little bit about the fruit when we read a previous devotional about peace. There are nine "fruits" talked about in Galatians 5:22–23. In fact—we're going to do something fun regarding this in a minute.

If you pray and ask God to help you (since we absolutely need His help all the time in every situation) to walk in His Spirit, it will definitely result in the self-control you're looking for. I also think you need to remember that we are all learning, and every day is one day closer to becoming more and more like Jesus.

Erin: Cam's right, you're not alone in this. You're in some really cool company. In Romans 7:15, the Apostle Paul himself said he shared the same struggle: "I do not understand what I do. For what I want to do I do not do, but what I hate I do." Now this is a guy who walked with God—I mean he wrote most of the New Testament, so if he struggled we're going to struggle too!

Thankfully he gave us some encouraging insight in verses 17–20 that explains what we all go through from time to time, "As it is, it is no longer I myself who do it, but it is sin living in me. For I know that good itself does not dwell in me, that is, in my sinful nature. For I have the desire to do what is good, but I cannot carry it out. For I do not do the good I want to do, but the evil I do not want to do—this I keep on doing. Now if I do what I do not want to do, it is no longer I who do it, but it is sin living in me that does it."

Sometimes what Paul was saying sounds like me. I don't do the good I want to do, but I keep on doing the things I don't want to do. Sheesh! It brings me peace to know some of this is normal for the Christian, that it's a struggle against sin living in me. I try to rest in the finished work of Christ and walk in the Spirit, and that's what I encourage you to do.

Dear friend, do not imitate what is evil but what is good. Anyone who does what is good is from God. Anyone who does what is evil has not seen God. —3 John 11

JUST FRUIT: No, not real fruit, like strawberries and grapes. YUMMY! But for the fun of trying to really learn and remember what God has shared with us in His Word, we're going to think fruit.

In the strawberry space provided for you, write down your top four favorite fruits. Then as you can see we have the Spirit fruit as well. Look up the verse we talked about in Galatians 5:22-23. List all the fruit mentioned here and then write down what you think each fruit means and why it's important for you to have it in your life.

Bah-ha-ha! I'm laughing so hard right now just thinking about this next **Cam Clip.** We thought it would be fun to talk about fruit and the Fruit of the Spirit with some of our friends. Check it out.

⎙ CAM CLIPS CODE: FRUIT

Favorite Fruit:

1.

2.

3.

4.

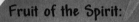

Fruit of the Spirit:

1.

2.

3.

4.

5.

6.

7.

8.

9.

Why do we let the world teach us how to live rather than follow after God's heart? It's so hard to be pure and stay focused on Jesus. Any thoughts on this, girls? —*Cassie*

Cam: Ya know what? You're right; it is hard to be pure and stay focused on Jesus. One of the things that comes to my mind is that we are in a real battle. I'm just a young girl, like you. I only know so much, which doesn't seem like very much at all most of the time. But I'm familiar with a couple of Scriptures that might help with your question.

We're sort of fighting against the things in this world, just like it says in 1 John 2:16, "For everything in the world—the lust of the flesh, the lust of the eyes, and the pride of life—comes not from the Father but from the world." And on top of it all the devil (yeah, I don't like even mentioning his name—EWW!) is constantly trying to mess us up, just as it says in Ephesians 6:12, "For our struggle is not against flesh and blood, but against the rulers, against the authorities, against the powers of this dark world and against the spiritual forces of evil in the heavenly realms."

With all this stuff going on we absolutely must follow and focus on Jesus. Because here's the deal—HE already won the great battle. When we belong to Him, we can overcome anything!

Erin: We do have a lot in this world that tries to go against us, but like the **Sweet Truth** says, "If God is for us, who can be against us?" He has given us His Spirit, so we can walk in the power of Jesus and the world can't push us around. And of course, put on the full armor of God and learn to use the sword of the Spirit (the Word of God) so we can stand against the enemy (Ephesians 6:13–17). There are so many more things we can do to live out our Christian life, things like prayer, Bible study, and devotional time (like this COOL *HCWG* devo you're doing right now). All these things help us to stay pure and focused on our first love—Jesus!

What, then, shall we say in response to these things? If God is for us, who can be against us? —Romans 8:31

LOVE JAM: What is "Love Jam"? Bah-ha-ha! We have no idea. But let's make it something suppa sweet. Let's write a love letter to Jesus. Plaster your paper or whatever you choose to write on with tons of hearts—like stickers and cool stuff. Tell Jesus why you love Him, how cool you think He is, and how thankful you are for Him and all He has done for you. When you're finished with your letter, put it in an envelope and seal the outside with a lipstick kiss. Then you might want to put your love letter in a safe place, like in your Bible or a secret drawer or someplace like that.

Well, I thought it might be cool to share my LOVE JAM with you. ☺ I'm sort of feeling shy about this, but as I've said in the past—if I share my heart with you maybe you'll share yours with me. Let's go!

CAM CLIPS CODE: LOVE LETTER

I'm jealous of my friend for a lot of reasons. I don't want to be envious of her looks and her talents, but I am. How can I stop this? —*Chelsea*

Cam: WOW! Not only do I LOVE your honesty, but the fact that you want to change and be the best you can be for Jesus and your friends—THAT JUST ROCKS. You've taken the first step, and it's a big one: fessing up—telling it like it is, girl! If you don't own it, how can you change it? Right? You're in God's hands, and He wants to deal with that jealousy and envy stuff.

Galatians 2:20 says, "I have been crucified with Christ and I no longer live, but Christ lives in me. The life I now live in the body, I live by faith in the Son of God, who loved me and gave himself for me." When I put that with 2 Corinthians 5:17, "Therefore, if anyone is in Christ, the new creation has come: The old has gone, the new is here!" it's ALL GOOD. You have everything you need to make this happen in your life. You have Jesus and He is enough. You want to change, and that's huge—so let God do the changing and you hang on to Him. Got that?

Erin: Jealousy and envy are things we all struggle with from time to time, but remember, GOD isn't finished with you yet! He's at work in your life right this very minute.

We're all human and we all fall, but by God's grace, we get back up again, accept His forgiveness, and keep walking with the Lord. What amazing news it is to know that you will never walk alone. NEVER! God is with you, and He will help you overcome all of this and more.

You also have the Word of God to help

you. It's your weapon when things like this happen. Run to God and His Word with all of this, and He will help you flush out the lies with truth. You see, it's like the enemy is lying to you and telling you that you need more to be happier—more of what your friend has. But you don't have to fall for the junk he's dishing out. Turn to Jesus. Let the truth of who He is refresh your memory.

Oh, and another great thing you should consider doing when you feel jealousy sneaking in on you—start thanking God. Thank Him for all that He is and all that He has done for you. A heart full of thanksgiving has no room for jealousy.

The weapons we fight with are not the weapons of the world. On the contrary, they have divine power to demolish strongholds. We demolish arguments and every pretension that sets itself up against the knowledge of God, and we take captive every thought to make it obedient to Christ.
—2 Corinthians 10:4–5

Sweet Section

9

School, music, bullies, and boys—life stuff we think about

I am always bullied at school, even by people who I think are my friends. What should I do? —*Kaykay*

Cam: My first thought about this is to pray. You should pray for the person who has been bullying you. Pray specifically for this person's heart. Bullying is a heart problem. Oftentimes people try to build themselves up by putting others down because of the way they feel about themselves. It's wrong and against God's will to bully others.

God looks at the *heart,* and He is watching; He sees what's going on in your life right now. He cares about you. Talk to Him about all of this. Praying for the person who hurts you is not easy, but Jesus told us to do just that. Luke 6:27 says, "'But to you who are listening I say: Love your enemies, do good to those who hate you.'" Ask God to help you pray for the person bullying you. I know this sounds crazy, but God's ways are not like our ways. He tells us that we should love our enemy. Most people would say you're crazy if you love the person who hurts you or hates you. But God's plan is always better.

I also think you should tell your parents and teachers about this bully. People who bully others need help. They *need* love; they need God!

Erin: Well, if people who you think are your friends are bullying you, then they are not your true friends ("A friend loves at all times," Proverbs 17:17). You need friends who will be an encouragement to you. People who build you up, not bring you down.

God will help you to have the kind of friends you need in your life right now. Ask Him to bring genuine friends into your life—friends who will help you grow closer to Him and genuinely care about you.

You also need to pray for the bully, like Cam suggested. Even though it might be very hard, it's important for you to pray for those who are mean to you. Doing this helps you and your heart. You don't want to hold unforgiveness and anger in your heart because it only ends up hurting you, just as it says in Ephesians 4:26–27, "'In your anger do not sin': Do not let the sun go down while you are still angry, and do not give the devil a foothold."

When I was in middle school, some boys in my class teased me relentlessly. I wouldn't say they bullied me, but I still felt really hurt by the things they said. Eventually it got better, but for a while it really bothered me a lot.

I prayed for them.

And my dad even came into school during lunch and sat at their table. He had words with all of the boys. He wasn't mean, but he made sure they understood how important it is to treat girls with respect.

You see, it's easy to love people who are nice to you, but it costs to love those who hurt and bully you. Remember this: The darker it is, the brighter your light shines, and where God guides He will provide. If you're being guided through a season that includes bullies, God will give you the grace to rise above it as you do right. Stay tough in the Lord!

I'm telling you to love your enemies. Let them bring out the best in you, not the worst. When someone gives you a hard time, respond with the energies of prayer, for then you are working out of your true selves, your God-created selves. —Matthew 5:44 (*The Message*)

⎔ CAM CLIPS CODE: BULLY

Every single girl in my class calls me fat! I try to go on diets. And lunch is the worst! If I go to take

a bite of something all the girls start to laugh at me and say mean things like, "I thought you were on a diet." What should I do? One day my best friend called me a hippo! My best friend did! What should I do? —*Sadgirl*

Cam: This is terrible and so hurtful. If this happened to me, I would probably tell my mother as soon as possible. She usually has just the right words to help me with stuff like this. Okay—so no matter what people say about your body, God sees your heart and that's what really matters. He sees that your heart is hurting when people say these mean things. He wants you to know that He hears what these people are saying and He doesn't like it. He made you exactly how He wanted you to be.

When people make fun of you and say nasty things about your body, it's like they're saying that God didn't do a good job of creating you. Yikes! You need to pray that God would open up their hearts and minds so these people (especially your best friend) see how their words hurt and that God doesn't like it when hurtful words come out of our mouths.

For whatever reason, these people are acting really unkind. The truth is that no matter how any of us appear, what we are inside always matters more than what we look like outside. We can't do anything about what others choose to do or say, but we can make sure our words are filled with the right things.

Erin: Words hurt! We can either use our words to encourage others or bring them down. I can only imagine how hard it is to hear even your best friend say something so hurtful. I've learned that sometimes those closest to us are the ones who can hurt us the most.

No matter what anyone says, **YOU ARE LOVED BY GOD JUST THE WAY YOU ARE!** (*Make sure you check out the* **Cam Clip** *video called Just the Way You Are.*) In the Bible it says that you are "fearfully and wonderfully made" by God (Psalm 139). Jesus made you just the way you are, and everything He has made is wonderful and beautiful!

We all need to know and receive the love God has for us so when other people hurt us (especially our closest friends) we can trust God to handle it. You see, unfortunately people are going to say mean things about how we look, what we wear, and all that kind of stuff. But God knows our hearts, and we can trust Him with the hurt that people cause us.

I know it's hard, but you need to ask God to help you to be thankful for how you look right now. You also need to ask Him to help you to forgive the people who said these things to you. Believe me, this is not easy at all. But if you go to God with all of this **HE WILL HELP YOU**!

As hard as it is, you need to ask God to help you forgive. When you forgive it doesn't mean that what these people did is okay. You forgive because God says you should and it will keep your heart from growing hateful.

Remember, this world places a lot of value on the way things look, instead of the way things are. It's one thing to *look* beautiful, but it's another thing altogether to actually *be* beautiful.

We all need Jesus!

This is one of my absolute favorite **SWEET TRUTHS**! In fact, this is the verse I use whenever I sign *HCWG* books. So AWESOME!

For you created my inmost being; you knit me together in my mother's womb. I praise you because I am fearfully and wonderfully made; your works are wonderful, I know that full well. —Psalm 139:13–14

✏️✨ Journal It Okay, so we need to get some things out on paper here. You need to pray about, think about, and write down all of the things about yourself that you're thankful for. For example, the first thing people notice when they see me (Camryn) is how tall I am. It's the first thing people usually say to me. I used to get so annoyed but not anymore. Instead, I remind myself to thank God for the way He created me. So get listing, girl. There are things about you—not just your outward appearance, but the inside you—that make you, YOU! List these special things that make you who you are—and thank God!

How can you still be a modest girl when all the stores and TV are showing such bad outfits to wear and all your friends are wearing them? —*Katelynn*

Cam: Well, you sort of answered that question yourself —or at least started to. You already understand that they are "bad outfits," and that's something every girl our age has to figure out because these days almost anything goes. I'm glad to hear that you see those outfits for what they are.

It sounds like you're struggling with peer pressure. You might have to decide what's more important: what your friends think or what the Lord thinks is best for you. Who would you rather dress to impress, your friends or God? Do you really want to wear bad outfits, or is it that you don't want your friends to make fun of what you wear? And one last thing (from my heart to yours), who are you going to listen to, your friends or God?

I'll be praying you make the right choice; it seems like you really want to choose modesty. I say, **GO FOR IT**!

Erin: First, I think it's great that dressing modestly matters to you; this really encourages me.

Rock on, girl, and hang in there—don't let anyone pressure you into being someone you don't want to be! Peer pressure can be awful and get us to make decisions we regret for a long time. I've been there. If all your friends are wearing bad outfits do you think they would really hate you if you dressed modestly? I mean, if they did I'd really question their friendship. There have got to be some really cool clothes out there that aren't inappropriate, and I'm willing to bet you have plenty in your closet.

I try to just dress to honor God and follow what I know is right instead of following what everyone else might be wearing. I encourage you to press on and continue to set a godly example for your friends.

Sweet Truth

I also want the women to dress modestly, with decency and propriety, adorning themselves, not with elaborate hairstyles or gold or pearls or expensive clothes, but with good deeds, appropriate for women who profess to worship God. —1 Timothy 2:9-10

Why do bad things happen? —*angel*

Cam: This is probably the hardest question and the most difficult to answer. I also think that it would be safe to say that every human being on this enormous planet has asked this very thing.

We've all asked this question at some point because we all experience bad things. For me, it's kind of weird because the worst thing that happened to me is actually one of the best things that has happened in my life too—the life and death of my older brother, Hunter.

Ugh, just thinking about him makes me cry. But I cry sad tears and happy tears. Sad—because I miss him every single day. Happy—because I know that I will see him again.

I'm going to let my sissy take over now, because to be honest with you, it's hard to answer this one, and I know she's older and has more wisdom than I do.

Erin: Thanks for the confidence, Cam, but there's really no easy answer to this question. It would take a lot more than a devotional to try and explain everything. And even after that, God has only revealed certain things to us through His Word. What we need to know He has told us. With everything else we just need to trust Him. He is God!

So, what I do know is this; God is absolutely good, all the time. Evil and bad things exist in our world because of sin. The amazing thing is that God chose to do something about our sin—because no matter what we do we can never be good enough to cleanse our hearts from the sin problem. God did something by sending His Son, Jesus, here—to rescue and save us. When we recognize our need for a Savior because of our own sin and choose to trust Him to save us, we become children of God.

I could go on and on about all of this.

Bottom line, bad exists because people choose to sin.

But the good news is that God doesn't leave us in our sin. He frees us from it through Jesus.

One more thing: Bad things don't stop happening when you become a follower of Jesus. What happens is that God gives you His heart so you can see your circumstances differently and trust God with everything (especially the things you don't understand) more and more each day!

I hope this helps!

Sweet Truth

"For my thoughts are not your thoughts, neither are your ways my ways," declares the LORD. **"As the heavens are higher than the earth, so are my ways higher than your ways and my thoughts than your thoughts."** —Isaiah 55:8–9

I am going into middle school, and I don't want to get caught up in the wrong crowd. I'm very nervous that I won't fit in. —*Dominique*

Cam: First of all, the fact that you care about this says a lot about the person you are— you're concerned and you want to do what's right. Awesome! I understand to some extent about the wrong-crowd thing. Even in a Christian school, people are people and cliques unfortunately happen. The thing is, you have to decide who you are and who God has called you to be. Don't be someone you're not just to try and fit in! It's not always easy, but it's the best plan.

Pray about making good, strong, godly friendships, and don't get caught up in any crowds. It's more important to fit in with who God made you to be and His plan for your life.

Like my daddy always says, "You are who you hang with." If you seek to love and know God more, He will lead you into all the right places He wants you to be—including meeting the right people in middle school. So don't be nervous. Pray and trust God to figure it all out for you.

Erin: I'm totally with Cam on this one. Do not get involved in cliques, be yourself, pray, study hard. You only go to middle school once, enjoy it. Do your best, and let God take care of the rest.

I used to get nervous about fitting in too, but I've learned to let the Word of God be my guide. The Bible tells me in Romans 8:31, "What, then, shall we say in response to these things? If God is for us, who can be against us?" So I just focus on following God, pleasing Him, not people—He is for me, so whatever life throws at me I know I'm not going to face it alone.

Sweet Truth

Do not be misled: "Bad company corrupts good character."
—1 Corinthians 15:33

Walk with the wise and become wise, for a companion of fools suffers harm. —Proverbs 13:20

What is your advice on music? Is it okay to listen to non-Christian music and still follow God? —*anonymous*

Cam: What a great question. Hmm, I'm sure my mother would like to answer this one. For a very long time, like the first ten years of my life, I was only allowed to listen to Christian music. Maybe I shouldn't say "allowed" because it's just that we didn't listen to anything else. In fact, I didn't even know about all the other types of music.

It was when I was around eleven years old that my sister and I were introduced to other types of music, like pop and country. I'm a huge country music fan, and I really like dance-type music too—because, girl, I love dancing!

I think God loves music. All throughout the Bible (especially in the Old Testament) you read about people playing music, singing, dancing, and celebrating the greatness of God. As long as the music you're listening to encourages you in the Lord and your walk with Him, then it's okay. I also think some music is just beautiful with a good message, and even though the song isn't a Christian song, it still blesses God because He created the beauty in it.

I hope I explained that okay. If not, my sister will.

Erin: Cam did a great job explaining her answer, but I'll go a bit deeper. Here's the thing, God cares about every single detail of our lives. EVERY. SINGLE. DETAIL. Including the music we listen to and the things we watch. And it's not like you can hide from God. He sees and knows everything. He knows us better than we know ourselves, and He tells us what's best for us in order to live a life that pleases Him.

If you don't care about pleasing God, then listen to whatever music you want to listen to. But if honoring God is important to you, then you need to be very careful about what you allow into your heart and mind.

That being said, if you're close to God, you'll know as soon as a song comes on whether or not you should continue listening to it. I know, I know, some songs are catchy and fun to listen to, but the message truly sucks any good right out of the song. It's your choice. No, you're not going to choose right every time, but the closer you get to Jesus, the more you'll long to honor and please Him. I hope this helps!

By the way, I'm a huge fan of Christian music, but there are some great songs out there that aren't Christian. I listen to them, and I honestly think that God is okay with it.

Oh—and one more thing. If your parents tell you that you can only listen to certain music: DO WHAT THEY SAY—AND OBEY. Seriously, even though you might disagree with them, you need to honor your parents first and foremost—everything else, like music and stuff, is not important by comparison.

Sweet Truth

Summing it all up, friends, I'd say you'll do best by filling your minds and meditating on things true, noble, reputable, authentic, compelling, gracious—the best, not the worst; the beautiful, not the ugly; things to praise, not things to curse.
—Philippians 4:8 (*The Message*)

Just Cool

Since we're talking about music, we thought it would be fun to write a song. Yes, that's right. Create your own song. If you can play an instrument, add some music too. Sometimes songs are written because of things that happen in a person's life. Be creative. We already have the space right here for you to write. Oh, and feel free to share your song by sending it to us through the *HCWG* website. If you'd like us to post your song on the website for all to see, we can do that too. How sweet!

OF COURSE we wrote a song! Check it out!

♫ CAM CLIPS CODE: MUSIC

I think I'm obsessed with Justin Bieber. I think about him a lot and have posters of him plastered all over my bedroom walls. Do you think this is a problem? —*JBLuver*

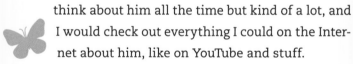

Cam: You're a girl I can so relate to! One of the walls in my bedroom is covered with Justin posters. I guess for a while I was sort of obsessed with him too. I didn't think about him all the time but kind of a lot, and I would check out everything I could on the Internet about him, like on YouTube and stuff.

Eventually, and this might sound rude—I got over him. Seriously, the excitement of all things Justin Bieber faded away, and I got over him. Yeah, of course I still think he's cute—well, suppa gorgeous is more like it—but my mind and heart are no longer consumed with thoughts of him.

I think it's normal to like a celebrity. It's so weird because we think we know these people when we don't know them at all. We see people, like Justin, and we start to like them (or think we do) because they're really cute (or in Justin Bieber's case— "suppa gorgeous") or because they can sing or play sports or whatever. So basically, we don't even like the person for who he really is but for what we see on the outside. Everything gets all mixed up when we focus on what the world looks at rather than the heart and the things of God.

Erin: Girlfriend! Don't worry—this is a typ- ical girl thing. Everyone has his or her celebrity crush. I think it's very cool that you're open and honest about thinking that you might have a JB obsession. I imag- ine that hundreds, if not thousands, of girls are in the same boat.

To get right to the point—Jesus is our first love. When He's not first in our hearts and lives, everything else in life gets all messed up. Sooo, no need to fret, just talk to Jesus about all of this. Ask God to help you to love HIM more than anyone or anything else. In fact, pray for Justin too.

One more thing. When you love Jesus with all your heart, He will bring the right boy into your life at just the right moment.

The simple believe anything, but the prudent give thought to their steps.
—Proverbs 14:15

I'm definitely not the coolest or prettiest girl in school, and I don't have a lot of friends. How do I try to fit in when I don't? —*Lonely Girl*

Cam: Hmm, okay, I'm a big fan of reality—and if you don't think you "fit in," just be sure you don't try and be someone you're not in order to fit in! Maybe you're not the "coolest" or "prettiest" girl, and maybe you don't have "a lot of friends"—but "coolness, beauty, and friendship" can really be traps if we make them our focus instead of God and what He desires for us.

Think of it this way: If the whole school thinks you're cool, but God isn't impressed, you've got a problem! And if the reality is that God created you for an extraordinary life, then you'll *never* fit into an ordinary life. (Oh that was a GOOD one, CAM!) Here's another Cam thought for you—maybe you're not supposed to fit in because you were created to stand out.

Let's let go of our desire to be accepted by "man" and seek after God's heart, where we are already cool, pretty, and loved like crazy.

Erin: Hmm, there are a lot of thoughts running through my mind about this. First of all, I would suggest that you try not to place a whole lot of importance on the approval of others and remember that what a person *seems to be* can be misleading. So don't try too hard to fit in, but just be who you are instead. If you do, I'm confident that you'll attract the same kind of people—people who will appreciate and accept you for who you are rather than how cool or pretty you can seem to be. Focus on walking in good character, treating others the way you want to be treated, and above all else, loving the Lord. Be true to who you are before the Lord, and let the rest of the world worry about fitting in with you.

Sweet Truth

Fear of man will prove to be a snare, but whoever trusts in the LORD is kept safe. —Proverbs 29:25

All of my friends have boys that they like. Is it wrong that I haven't really liked a boy yet? How will I know when a boy is the right one for me?
—Cherish

Cam: First, and this is HUGE, the fact that you care whether or not it is wrong to have not really liked a boy yet sets you apart from most girls. Just know that, okay? I'm really impressed—there are not a lot of girls our age who would even consider the question, let alone honestly ask it! Way to go! And speaking of honesty, I can't think of a situation where it would be wrong to be honest with yourself—that actually seems to be the real issue here! You "haven't really liked a boy yet"—even though all of your friends have boys that they like. So rather than get with the program and do what your friends are doing, you'd rather remain "without" and wait for the right guy! AWESOME! There is nothing even remotely wrong with that, or the fact that you simply haven't felt that deeply for a guy yet. I'd be willing to bet that a lot of kids our age actually feel like you do but simply do what everyone else is doing and go out with a guy just because.

Erin: So if I understand you correctly, your question is twofold: You're not sure if it may actually be wrong that you haven't or don't like a boy yet? And the second part of your dilemma would be how are you going to know when the right boy comes along? The fact that all your friends have boys that they like and you don't just means that you are being true to yourself—period!

I think you're definitely doing the right thing by keeping it real and not rushing into a relationship for the sake of a relationship. There is nothing wrong with your not liking a guy romantically yet, and everything right with waiting for the feelings to come.

As far as how you know when the right guy comes into your world—I'm not exactly an experienced columnist and have a long way to go before I release "Dear Erin" ☺. Based on my limited experience (I do have a boyfriend right now. I wasn't allowed to date until I turned seventeen. I'm thankful that I waited. Sorry, I'm getting sidetracked and this is all talk for another time), which is supported by a fair amount of Bible study, I'd say there's more of a God connection with a guy.

There are practical things you can look for such as a deep relationship with the Lord, seriousness about school, kindness, honesty, and things like that. But even all of this could line up and yet the relationship could be missing the "God connection." It's really important—and the best way I can put it is that "you know when you know."

Keep your priorities where they should be, meaning, be about the Father's business and following Jesus—and He will take care of the boy business. As you serve Him, love Him, and allow Him to do what only He can do in every area of your life, you'll find that He really does know what He's doing. He'll bring the right guy, in the right way, at the right time, as long as your heart and life are right with Him.

Sweet Truth

But seek first his kingdom and his righteousness, and all these things will be given to you as well. —Matthew 6:33

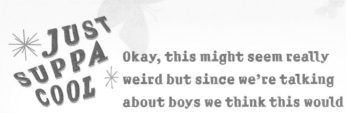

JUST SUPPA COOL

Okay, this might seem really weird but since we're talking about boys we think this would be such a great thing to do. Write a letter to your future husband. WHAT? We know, it sounds crazy. So let's just do it anyway ☺.

Your letter can be a prayer, like all the things that you would pray about for him, even though you don't even know this boy yet. This is actually very cool if you think about it.

Just imagine, if you do this and then keep it, you can give this to your future husband on your wedding day. Goose bumps! How adorable! It's not a bad thing to plan ahead and what a cool gift this letter or prayer would be. Suppa cool!

There are a lot of people in my school that don't believe in God, and they swear a lot. I want to tell them about Jesus, but I'm afraid if I start talking to them they will get mad or make fun of me or something like that. What should I do? —*Courtney*

Cam: Girlfriend—I'm totally cheering you on right now for caring enough to ask the question and be so honest about the way you feel too. Wow! It can be scary to share the love of God, especially with people who seem really unloving. The thing is, not everyone will put you down for sharing the Gospel, but it does happen! In other countries there are people suffering for what we believe, but here getting mocked is usually as bad as it gets for most of us.

One of the things that helps is to just make up your mind ahead of time that you might get put down for sharing your faith. That classmates might reject you and may even hate you! But remember, it's not you they reject, it's Jesus. He said, "If the world hates you, keep in mind that it hated me first" (John 15:18). But you know we all sometimes cover up the way we really feel to hide our fears and insecurities. If you pray for the boldness to live out Christ's love, there are those who really hurt that will find you—God will lead them to you. And you might just have the joy of bringing them to Jesus. Now THAT'S worth being made fun of—don't you think?

Erin: Absolutely, there will be those who get angry, those who would rather run from the light of life. John 3:19–20 talks about them, "This is the verdict: Light has come into the world, but people loved darkness instead of light because their deeds were evil. Everyone who does evil hates the light, and will not come into the light for fear that their deeds will be exposed." You sort of have to settle it ahead of time; you know, count the cost up front and go for it.

I have found that friendship is one of the most honest and powerful ways to touch people with the love of Jesus. Treating others with love and respect, and having their back, will earn a trust that is worth more than even the best preaching. People are looking for love and meaning—and those can be found through relationships. There's a saying that's really cool that goes something like this, "People don't care how much you know, until they know how much you care."

Remember though, it's a life of faith we're supposed to live, and faith is "being sure of what we hope for and certain of what we do not see" (Hebrews 11:1). We trust in the God we cannot see, but we share a Gospel, build a kingdom, and live a life of love so others can see Jesus. We share our confidence in what is hoped for and the assurance of what is unseen as we live out our faith.

So I guess you just might need to make up your mind now, that just as Jesus was rejected (Isaiah 53:3), His servants might be as well—but that's okay. Better to be accepted by God and rejected by man, if necessary, than the other way around.

One more thing. Remember, the greatest privilege we have as followers of Jesus is to tell others about Him—to tell the lost the only Way to be found!

Then Jesus came to them and said, "All authority in heaven and on earth has been given to me. Therefore go and make disciples of all nations, baptizing them in the name of the Father and of the Son and of the Holy Spirit, and teaching them to obey everything I have commanded you. And surely I am with you always, to the very end of the age." —Matthew 28:18-20

There's this boy I like. He's not a Christian, but he's really nice. I don't know if he likes me. Please help! —*ChatterBox*

Cam: Oh boy...I'm not really one to give out relationship advice since I'm not even allowed to start dating until I turn seventeen. I don't think you're talking about dating, just liking this boy. Right? Here's the thing, just because someone isn't a Christian doesn't mean he can't be a great guy. The big problem here—like seriously—is the fact that you are both going in different directions spiritually...in your heart.

I don't know if I'm making sense, but if you're a believer, the problem is that an unbeliever lives like the rest of the world, probably doing a lot of the things you are against. It can really mess with your relationship with the Lord and get between you and God. It doesn't mean it can never work, but what's easier: if you stand on a chair and try to pull a guy up onto it—or if he tries to pull you down?

My advice would be to just be friends. Get to know each other. Show him what living for Jesus looks like. If you really care about him, you're gonna want him to know Jesus. Always put God first in whatever you do!

Erin: Great advice, Cam! I'll add a couple things. If this guy doesn't know the Lord yet, he's going to automatically follow after the things of this world. He really doesn't know any better because the Holy Spirit isn't in him, so his values are going to totally clash with yours. He will be following the things of this world while you choose not to as a Christian.

It's a really hard decision, but the chair concept that Cam shared is good; it's a lot easier to be pulled down than pull someone else up. Pray for him, share with him, but guard your heart carefully. The **Sweet Truth** below may not seem especially sweet right now, but following it could keep you from a broken heart or falling away from Jesus.

And one more thing. Sometimes we like a boy and we just can't help it. Right? Maybe he's really fun and cute or whatever. Here's the deal: If you can't help it, you can always pray about it. Talk to God about how you feel about this boy and let God lead you in the direction He wants you to go. And remember, God always has a good plan for you—no, a suppa-great plan!

Sweet Truth

Do not be yoked together with unbelievers. For what do righteousness and wickedness have in common? Or what fellowship can light have with darkness? What harmony is there

**between Christ and Belial? What does a believer
have in common with an unbeliever?**

—2 Corinthians 6:14-15

We're feeling the need to talk to
some boys. Yes, real boys! Let's
get right down to it and ask the
questions—like what do boys look for in a girlfriend
and how do you know if a boy likes you or not. This
should be very interesting!

CAM CLIPS CODE: BOY TALK

**The world nowadays is very tempting.
How do you have the courage to say no to
wrong things and yes to right things?** —*Tessa*

Cam: Wow, courage—you're right, it's really needed to
overcome the world and its temptations these days. And
seriously, getting serious about following Jesus is the best
way I know to find the courage we need. It's so much easier to give into temptations than to fight against them.

So where do we get the courage to live a godly life? From Jesus Himself! He's promised to be with us, to guide us, and to help us! In Acts 1:8, right before He went back to heaven, Jesus said, "'But you will receive power when the Holy Spirit comes on you; and you will be my witnesses in Jerusalem, and in all Judea and Samaria, and to the ends of the earth.'" He's given you the power through the Holy Spirit in you—believe it and receive it, girlfriend!

Erin: You said that right—the world nowadays is very tempting! I'm not exactly a Bible major, but I remember a passage in Hebrews that kind of speaks to your question. "By faith Moses, when he had grown up, refused to be known as the son of Pharaoh's daughter. He chose to be mistreated along with the people of God rather than to enjoy the fleeting pleasures of sin. He regarded disgrace for the sake of Christ as of greater value than the treasures of Egypt, because he was looking ahead to his reward" (Hebrews 11:24–26).

What really struck me about this is that Moses had it all—every temptation he wanted to yield to, he could because he was a part of Pharaoh's court. That must have in-cluded wealth and power galore! And yet, not only did he refuse to be known as

Pharaoh's grandson, but instead be connected with the very slaves his grandfather ruled over and made suffer. Ya gotta love this guy Moses!

So what does this have to do with courage and your question? Well, "He regarded disgrace for the sake of Christ as of greater value than the treasures of Egypt, because he was looking ahead to his reward." That's where you draw the courage from—living for Christ is more valuable than anything the world can offer. Why? Because the reward is up ahead—it's certain! Just as the passing of these worldly temptations—they might feel great for a short time, but they will pass away and so will we. We have to be strong and hang on to the truth that saying yes to right and no to wrong will honor God and bless us big-time in the end.

Sweet Truth

Be strong and very courageous. Be careful to obey all the law my servant Moses gave you; do not turn from it to the right or to the left, that you may be successful wherever you go. —Joshua 1:7

Sweet Section

3

BFFs, friends—and

figuring it all out

I told my friend that I didn't want to be her friend because she talks behind my back, but I really like her. What would you do? —*Alabama*

Cam: Well, if your friend talks behind your back, she's not a true friend. For instance, if you see your friend talking to another girl about you and you just want to burst into fury—DON'T DO IT! What you need to do right away is pray and ask God what to do. Even if this happens in school, go to the bathroom or wherever you can have a private prayer moment with God. If someone tells you that your friend is talking about you, you first need to go to that friend and ask her if it's true. I know if your friend talks about you, you just want to go up to her and get in her face about it. I know the feeling. But it says in Proverbs 17:17, "A friend loves at all times."

Even through the struggles, the ups and downs, your friend should always be there for you. I know you said that you really like her, but if she were a TRUE FRIEND, she wouldn't talk behind your back. The real deal here is to keep this relationship going, you'd have to pretend she wasn't talking behind your back. Not only would you have to pretend you didn't know, which involves lying to others, but you'd have to pretend you didn't care—that it was okay, meaning that you'd have to lie to yourself. You'd have to act like the whole relationship was something that it wasn't. NOT COOL!

Oh, but remember, if she asks you to forgive her, you need to forgive and move on, though I would imagine that it would take an awful lot for her to earn your trust back. And just to clear it up, trust and forgiveness are two very different things that are kinda easy to confuse. We always want to forgive when someone wrongs us—it frees our hearts and God commands us to (after all, He's forgiven us). But that doesn't mean we automatically trust them—that has to be earned over time.

Friendship is hard sometimes because no one is perfect but Jesus! We all need to ask Him for help to *be* a good friend and to bring good, godly friends into our lives.

Erin: Although I've not had to deal with this exact situation, I do know what it feels like to be hurt by friends. It's hard, really hard. Sometimes you realize that the people you thought were your closest friends are the ones who end up hurting you the most. The truth is, if this

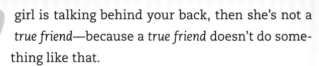

girl is talking behind your back, then she's not a *true friend*—because a *true friend* doesn't do something like that.

I would definitely try and work things out with her. In other words, talk to her about how you feel, explain that you know that she's been talking behind your back, and ask her why she's doing this. The Bible is very clear about this, check out Matthew 18:15, "'If your brother or sister sins, go and point out their fault, just between the two of you. If they listen to you, you have won them over.'" Maybe you'll end up having a great conversation that might strengthen your friendship. But maybe, you'll find out she doesn't care about how you feel when you share your heart with her.

In the end, you're going to have to make a decision as far as whether or not this is the type of friend you want to invest your heart in. Bear in mind, disappointment is something we all have to learn to deal with from time to time— it's part of life.

Sometimes relationships are only meant for a season—or a certain amount of time. Not all relationships last a lifetime, and that's totally okay. They are seasonal and seasons pass, it's really no one's fault.

We're all human with our ups and downs, goods and bads.

Also, I think it's important to pray. Jesus knows and cares about how you feel. He wants you to talk to Him about everything. He also wants you to BE a great friend as well as have great friends. He's the only one that knows everyone's hearts. He's the only one that can show you who your true friends are!

Sweet Truth

A friend loves at all times. —Proverbs 17:17

I told on my close friend for doing something bad, and now she doesn't want to be my friend. Was that a good choice to tell on her? —*Bobby*

Cam: For sure—this is a tough one. I probably would've talked to my friend before telling on her. I'm thinking that if you would have confronted her and given her the opportunity to own up, then she might have made whatever it was she did right on her own. It also might have kept your friendship from falling apart.

Then again, depending on what she did, telling on her might actually have helped her. Hmm. She probably doesn't want to be your friend anymore because she's mad about getting into trouble. She might need some time to realize on her own that she shouldn't have done what she did in the first place, and it was your concern that led you to do what you did. I'm just thinking out loud right now about all of this. If you told on your friend because you didn't know what else to do or because you didn't want her to continue to do the wrong thing, I guess you made the right choice. Ugh, I'm just not so sure, so let's see what Erin thinks.

Erin: Thanks for putting this one on me, Cam. Um, yeah. My initial response to this is similar to what Camryn suggested—I would've said something to my friend before telling on her. We don't know whether or not you did do this or if she was willing to listen to you if you did try to talk to her. Either way, allowing a friend to continue to make bad choices is not a good thing. A true friend would not want her friend to continue doing bad things, but remember, you aren't responsible for her choices—she is. Obviously, telling on her and getting other people involved should be a last resort, but depending on what's going on, eventually you may have to tell on her so she can get help and then she will hopefully stop doing bad.

Hopefully, someday she'll realize that you told on her because you care. I'm thinking that you might want to write your friend a letter. Tell her how much you care about her and ask her if she would consider being your friend again. And of course pray for her!

Sweet Truth

Wounds from a friend can be trusted, but an enemy multiplies kisses.

—Proverbs 27:6

How can I be a good example to my friends?
—Bella Boo

Cam: Okay, so the fact that you want to be a good example for your friends is very cool. This shows that you care about them and want what's best for them. We are all a work in progress every single day. Sometimes we get it right and some days we don't. Right? We can learn how to be a good example by looking at the way people we trust live their lives. Ha-ha-ha, I was just thinking that my mom is an awesome example for me, except when she puts mascara on when she's driving. Yikes. Seriously, God has placed role models in our lives for a reason—to teach us. But ultimately God is our perfect example. And we can learn all about Him through reading and studying the Bible. (If you're like me, those two words "reading" and "studying" probably make you cringe or scream. Ask God to help you get excited about reading His Word.)

Erin: Jesus is the perfect example for all of us. When we seek Him, we get to know and love Him more. The more we know and love Him, the more we long to live for Him—the way He has called us to live. I honestly think the only way to be a godly friend and good example is by getting to know Jesus more. His life, love, and example will flow out of our love for Him. Loving Him comes first. So focus on getting to know the Lord and He will help you to be a great example for your friends.

Sweet Truth

Don't let anyone look down on you because you are young, but set an example for the believers in speech, in life, in love, in faith and in purity. —1 Timothy 4:12

**SUPPA COOL** God created us to be in relationships—first with Him and then with other people. Friendships are important. Let's talk to some girls (and maybe a few boys—maybe) about what they think a good example looks like when it comes to friendships.

📷 CAM CLIPS CODE: GOOD EXAMPLE

How should I deal with feeling left out when my friends are all doing something bad that I don't think I should do? —*Angie*

Cam: Like my dad says, "If all your friends were jumping off a cliff, would you do it too?" (Hmm, maybe if I had a parachute attached to my back! Just kidding!) Of course I wouldn't be so stupid and crazy! Feeling left out is not easy and it hurts, especially when it's your friends who are ditching you. But here's the deal—doing what's right is more important than having a million friends who choose to do wrong. Got that? Your friends will probably get in trouble anyway, and then they'll wish they didn't do what they knew was wrong.

Erin: First of all, if you stand for what's right, you NEVER stand alone! God is with you! When everyone is doing what you know is wrong and you fall for the trap and join them—you're no better off than they are. However, when you choose to do right, especially when it's hard, God will bless you. He will strengthen you and give you the courage to stand firm.

One passage I hang on to when I find myself in that situation is Ephesians 6:12–13, it kind of brings me back to reality. "For our struggle is not against flesh and blood, but against the rulers, against the authorities, against the powers of this dark world and against the spiritual forces of evil in the heavenly realms. Therefore put on the full armor of God, so that when the day of evil comes, you may be able to stand your ground..." Yes, you might continue to feel left out by your friends, but eventually you'll learn and understand that the things you're missing out on are not worth it. Your friends are not more important than pleasing God by choosing to do the right thing. We should always choose to do the right thing—then we can rest knowing we've stayed true to what we know is right and pleasing to the Lord. We can just leave the results to God.

Sweet Truth **Whoever sows to please their flesh, from the flesh will reap destruction; whoever sows to please the Spirit, from the Spirit will reap eternal life. Let us not become weary in doing good, for at the proper time we will reap a harvest if we do not give up.** —Galatians 6:8-9

Prayer Time *It's time to pray right now for your friends. You can pray however you want but if it's okay we'd like to suggest just a few things to pray about. First of all, talk to God about everything that's going on with your friends. Give Him the details. Tell Him how you feel. Then, thank Him for your friends. Get specific. God has allowed certain people into your life for a reason. Pray about how you can learn from this situation with your friends.*

What should I do if none of my friends are Christians? —*Tegan*

Cam: Great question, and the fact that you are concerned about this shows a love for God that's really special. It shows a lot of wisdom (big word) too, because we become like those we hang out with. If someone moves down south, sooner or later you'll notice they begin to speak with a southern accent. Same with New York City—they'll talk like a "New Yokah." LOL. It's true! This reminds me, whenever I say that I'm from New York, people always think I live in New York City. I don't. In fact we live really far from the city. Anyway—back to you.

More important, our lives are often shaped by those we are close to and spend a lot of time with, so having the right people in our lives is super important. So get connected to a good youth group that can help strengthen your walk with God. Get involved and make Christian friends who share the same kind of love for Jesus.

On the other hand, continue to be a friend to your current friends for sure. Jesus said go into all the world and share the good news. Be strong in your faith. Don't stop talking to them, and don't stop praying for them. Let your light shine and be the difference, girl!

Erin: It sounds to me like you're right where God wants you to be. And though your friends aren't believers (yet!), your faith, grace, and godly character are sure to bring the reality of the love of God up close and personal. How are people going to know about Jesus if those whom He reigns in aren't there to be His hands and feet? So go to them and reach out to them—to bring His love to life!

Like Cam said, we also need fellowship so we can grow stronger in our faith and knowledge of God, but as the Apostle Paul pointed out in Romans 10:14, "How then shall they call on him in whom they have not believed? And how shall they believe in him of whom they have not heard? And how shall they hear without a preacher?" (NKJV). And that's you! Remember, God goes before you and He will help you be the witness you're called to be.

In the same way, let your light shine before men, that they may see your good deeds and praise your Father in heaven.
—Matthew 5:16

Just Cool

Let's get creative and maybe a little radical for a minute.

Imagine you've been given the opportunity to write a letter to your friend. This will be the very last thing she'll ever read. What will you say to her? Seriously, give this some thought and you should probably pray about it too. Then pick one of your friends (one who is not a Christian) and write her a letter. Tell her all the things you would want to say to her, knowing that your letter will be the very last words she will ever read. Wow!

When you're finished, put your letter in an envelope and start praying. Pray that God will tell you if and when you should give your friend the letter.

I want to share my letter with you. At first I was going to keep it to myself, but I think it will be cool if I share my heart with you. Check it out!

CAM CLIPS CODE: LETTER TO THE LOST

My friend always brings me down, calling me fat, ugly, and lame. What should I do? —Jodi

Cam: Ugh, seriously, no one should have to go through what you're dealing with. Words have power—they can build us up or bring us down. Proverbs 18:21 says, "The tongue has the power of life and death, and those who love it will eat its fruit." That kind of talk is super mean and hurtful, even if your friend is kidding around.

Pray for her, love and forgive her, but you should also confront her and absolutely tell her how she makes you feel. If she is truly your friend, she will apologize and stop talking to you like that.

Erin: Wow, this is not good. I'm wondering if maybe your friend is insecure about who she is and that's why she's always bringing you down. If she's truly your friend she wouldn't treat you this way. To always put you down also reflects a lot of pride, and that's never a good thing. Another thing you might consider is if this attitude is her normal, all-the-time attitude, sooner or later your friend is going to say the wrong thing to the wrong person, in the wrong way and the consequences could be pretty bad. Definitely draw a line and help her understand what she's doing.

Colossians 4:6 says, "Let your conversation be always full of grace, seasoned with salt, so that you may know how to answer everyone." Be sure you confront your friend with humility and kind words (even though it's hard—really hard—it's the most loving thing you can do).

My best friend always speaks her mind. Sometimes she can be so rude about it. Should I say something to her? —Lexi

Cam: I've known people who are—well, what would you call it?—overly honest, LOL. If it bothers you then, yes, you should try to talk to her. Be sure she knows you appreciate her honesty, but it's having a negative effect on you—ya know what I mean.

Think about Proverbs 15:1, "A gentle answer turns away wrath, but a harsh word stirs up anger." It sounds like her words are kind of harsh, and I don't think she wants to stir up anger, but if she's being rude, then her words will hurt. I'd talk to her. Unless of course you want me to talk to her...I wish I could, but this is for you to tackle, my friend. (Um, tackle because my dad used to be a football quarterback. Yeah!)

Erin: I agree. If she's honest to a fault, it's not just with you, and chances are she's rude to others as well. I'm sure her heart means well or you wouldn't be her friend to begin with. But even so, if our friends don't set us straight when we make mistakes, then who will? Definitely go to her privately and try to help her see that even though her heart might be in the right place, her way about it is totally off and she's hurting or offending people who mean a lot to her.

I was just thinking about the verse we chose for our **Sweet Truth**. It's so true; we should always look for the best in each other. Maybe this friend has qualities about her that are really great. You should encourage her in those things and trust God and pray about the other issues that bother you. In fact, after you read the **Sweet Truth**, we have something really cool you can do for your friend.

Sweet Truth

Be patient with each person, attentive to individual needs. And be careful that when you get on each other's nerves you don't snap at each other. Look for the best in each other, and always do your best to bring it out.
—1 Thessalonians 5:15 (*The Message*)

JUST TELL HER: So listen, no one is perfect. Right? Here's something you can do that might help ease the tension in your friendship. Write your friend a letter or send her a card (an *HCWG* card, of course) and tell her how thankful you are for her and your friendship. Point out the things about her that make her shine. ☺ Hey, and if you do this—tell us about it. We want to know how it all went down, so send us a message at the website.

My super-best friend is really insecure and looks down on herself. What can I say or do to encourage her? —*Ella*

Cam: Everyone needs a friend like you! God bless you for caring enough to want to make a difference and be a good friend. My first thought is that your friend doesn't see herself as God sees her, so you've got to point her to His love and promises. And then you can encourage her and help her believe who she is in Christ.

A great verse to share with her is 2 Corinthians 5:17, "Therefore, if anyone is in Christ, he is a new creation; the old has gone, the new has come!" God sees her as a new person, and then as that new person, she can do anything she puts her mind to—anything God calls her to do. Philippians 4:13 promises, "I can do all this through Christ who gives me strength."

WHOA...Scripture overload—watch out!

Erin: How cool is it that no matter what's going on in our lives, God sees us as victorious through Christ? In Him we can overcome the challenges life throws at us, instead of being defeated and crushed by life's trials. Gideon was hiding from the enemy when God called him, hiding out so he wouldn't be seen. Look at what the Angel of the Lord said: "When the angel of the LORD appeared to Gideon, he said, 'The LORD is with you, mighty warrior'" (Judges 6:12). He sure didn't feel like a mighty warrior or see himself that way at that point—but in time he learned to, and your friend will too. With lots of encouragement from God's Word, the Bible, your example and friendship, and prayer, she will change. She'll find her victorious identity as a new creation—the young lady God has called her to be—and it will overcome the lies she believes about herself now.

Sweet Truth

Delight yourself in the LORD and he will give you the desires of your heart.
—Psalm 37:4

SUPPA COOL Okay, so this is going to be really fun, sort of like a secret-agent kind of thing. Your friend needs some encouragement, right? Well, let's go undercover and do the best we can to help her. Here's what you'll need before we get started: five 3x5-inch cards, tape, colored markers, cool stickers, and your creative ability and heart. Are you ready? Great! We've picked out five Scriptures that we think will really bless your super-best friend; they're listed below.

Take your 3x5-inch cards and write one verse on each card. Leave room on the back of the card to write her a personal note. Something from your heart to encourage her. Now get crafty and decorate your cards. Go all out, girl!

Okay, so the next time you're over at your friend's house, hide these encouragement notes so she'll discover them at different times. Like hide one in her dresser drawer. Maybe tape one to her bathroom mirror or in her closet. If she's reading a book, you could place a card in her book like a bookmark. You'll do great! Have fun!

"I praise you because I am fearfully and wonderfully made; your works are wonderful, I know that full well." —Psalm 139:14

"For he will command his angels concerning you to guard you in all your ways." —Psalm 91:11

"The LORD your God is with you, he is mighty to save. He will take great delight in you; he will quiet you with his love, he will rejoice over you with singing." —Zephaniah 3:17

"The LORD himself goes before you and will be with you; he will never leave you nor forsake you. Do not be afraid; do not be discouraged." —Deuteronomy 31:8

"You can be sure that God will take care of everything you need..." —Philippians 4:19 (The Message)

A good friend of mine whom I pray for and keep close to my heart is being distracted by her boyfriend. This boy even got her into doing some really bad things. What can I do? —*Susie*

Cam: That's a tough one. I don't have a lot of experience with this, but of course the Bible has some good advice. The warning is pretty clear in 2 Corinthians 6:14, "Do not be yoked together with unbelievers. For what do righteousness and wickedness have in common? Or what fellowship can light have with darkness?" If your friend doesn't know Jesus, she really doesn't know any better. She's just going to go along with what everyone else—specifically her boyfriend—is doing. You're already doing the best thing—praying! Don't stop!

This question makes me think of the story Jesus told about the Prodigal Son and how he eventually "came to his senses" (Luke 15:17) and turned his life back in the right direction. If you've never read this story before, you should, because it's awesome. Whatever you can do to help your friend come to her senses—do it. You can't force her to want what is right for her, but you can let her know she is loved for who she is regardless of the things she may do. And I'll say it again; PRAY, PRAY, PRAY for her.

Erin: The influence a romantic relationship has on us is powerful, which is why the Bible is so clear about getting involved with people who share our faith and values. I would say to pray like crazy for your friend and try to keep the lines of communication open. Stay strong in your faith and continue to be a loving example that will win her heart back to what she knows is right.

For where your treasure is, there your heart will be also. —Matthew 6:21

I have a lot of friends who make fun of me because I'm a Christian. They always say they don't understand. What should I do? —*Julia*

Cam: I'm sorry you get made fun of for your faith; that's not cool at all—and it's not very "friendly." Before we even get started, you need to know something that just might encourage you. Jesus got made fun of too—a lot. In fact even while He was hanging on the cross people would pass by Him and shout out mean things. You can read about all of this in the New Testament. What amazes me is the fact that Jesus could have shut the mouths of the people who made fun of Him—but He didn't. And when I say "shut the mouths," I mean He could've literally done whatever He wanted to in order to make them stop talking. Instead, He trusted His Father in heaven and He loved those people anyway. It's crazy, isn't it? Oh how I wish I could be more like Jesus!

The fact that your friends don't understand your faith is actually scriptural. (In other words, the

Bible talks about this happening to people who follow Jesus. See, I'm telling you, everything we need can be found in God's Book! Check it out, girl!)

1 Corinthians 2:14 says, "The person without the Spirit does not accept the things that come from the Spirit of God but considers them foolishness, and cannot understand them because they are discerned only through the Spirit." Hopefully this verse helps you understand why your friends don't get your love for God. To explain this Scripture the way I understand it, I'd say that the deal is that your friends don't know Jesus, and therefore the Holy Spirit doesn't live in their hearts. Because of this, they think stuff that has to do with God is weird—like it doesn't make sense to them because the Spirit of God isn't in them. I hope my explanation helped.

As far as what to do, keep living out and sharing what you believe and follow the **Sweet Truth**, Matthew 5:16, "In the same way, let your light shine before others, that they may see your good deeds and glorify your Father in heaven." And don't forget to keep praying for them.

Erin: Romans 8:5 is another great verse that might help you understand why your friends are acting like this,

"Those who live according to the flesh have their minds set on what the flesh desires; but those who live in accordance with the Spirit have their minds set on what the Spirit desires."

Ya see, there's like this unseen battle of the heart going on between your friends and you that can't be helped if they don't know the Lord. They're going to react negatively to your faith mainly because their minds and hearts are focused on the things of this world instead of godly things. That doesn't mean that their making fun of you is okay, just because they don't get it. No way! The best thing to do is what Cam said, live out your faith, pray for them, and let your light shine.

Oh, and one more thing to remember: When they make fun of you, they're making fun of God too. And as you can imagine, this doesn't please Him at all. When you respond to their treatment in a way they might expect, like talking back to them in order to stick up for yourself, it will probably make matters worse. But if you choose to respond in love (which is sometimes really hard) and remember that God will protect you, I think you'll see that the outcome will be much better.

In the same way, let your light shine before others, that they may see your good deeds and glorify your Father in heaven.
—Matthew 5:16

I don't have very many "real" friends. How can I make good friends? *—Ella*

Cam: Friends are very important. I don't know where I'd be without my close friends. And ya know what else is suppa cool? Jesus calls us His friends. (Check out the **Sweet Truth**!)

Hey, the Bible is full of verses that talk about friends and friendship. Proverbs 12:26 gives some good advice. It says, "The righteous choose their friends carefully, but the way of the wicked leads them astray." So definitely choose your friends carefully. You don't want to get close to anyone who doesn't have values like you do because he or she might cause you to make bad choices. (P.S.—Notice I said "he or she"—just a reminder that boys can actually be great friends too. In fact, right now I have a very close friend that's a boy, and it's cool being able to talk to him about stuff.)

One more thing. God knows your heart's desire. He wants you to have good, godly friends. Pray and trust Him to bring the right people into your life.

Erin: Friends are absolutely one of God's greatest blessings. Church is a great place to meet new people. There are usually youth groups and Sunday school classes that are organized by age so kids can hang out with other kids their age. When you're there just be a friend and participate—get involved in the activities and games that are offered. Another really GREAT way to connect is to volunteer to help when you can; there are never enough helpers to go around, and people tend to notice when you're willing to help.

And again, pray! I feel like we tell people to pray all the time but it really is the most important advice we could ever share. We need to talk to God about anything and everything. Prayer is talking to God. He wants what's best for you so talk to Him about this and He will guide and help you.

Sweet Truth

I no longer call you servants, because a servant does not know his master's

business. Instead, I have called you friends, for everything that I learned from my Father I have made known to you. —John 15:15

I made one of my best friends very upset. I said I was sorry, but she's still mad and won't talk to me. What if she never forgives me? —*Nikki*

Cam: First of all, I admire you (or, I think you ROCK!) for apologizing and trying to make things better. Whatever you did must have really hurt your friend, but if you're really sorry, have apologized and done all you can—then it's up to her now. Of course you can't force her to forgive you, since that's totally a work of God in her heart. But you can certainly pray about it. Pray that God will help your best friend to forgive and then let go and let God do what only He can do to make your relationship better again.

Listen, I'll tell you what I did when something similar happened to me. The very first thing I did was talk to my mom about it. After she helped me see how wrong I was, we prayed together. After that, I prayed some more and then I wrote my best friend a letter. I didn't just write the letter, I got face to face with my best friend and read what I wrote to her. It was all so hard. We cried and prayed, and I'm so thankful God worked everything out for us. It's weird; I actually think our friendship is stronger now.

Don't give up—give it all to God!

Erin: If she's one of your best friends, then no doubt this is hurting both of you. Like Cam said, you absolutely need to pray, especially since you've already asked her to forgive you. Pray that God would help you to be patient as He works in both of your hearts.

God's desire is always forgiveness. He doesn't want your friend to carry around a heart full of unforgiveness and anger. No matter what, God wants her to forgive, but it might take time. Trust that God will do all He can (since He's God—well, you can expect good things, right?) to help you and your friend. But really, your friend has to be willing to forgive you and leave the past in the past so you can both look to the future.

Life is short. We don't have time to hold grudges. Hopefully, God will move her heart, and she'll remember the good times and realize you're just human and can't do any more than apologize.

Then Peter came to Jesus and asked, "LORD, how many times shall I forgive my brother when he sins against me? Up to seven times?" Jesus answered, "I tell you, not seven times, but seventy-seven times."
—Matthew 18:21–22

Just Cool

So, like I shared above, I wrote my BFF a letter asking her to forgive me, and then I asked if we could get together, and when we did I read her the letter I wrote. I'm thinking a letter just might be a good thing for you to do. And since you've already asked her to forgive you, maybe you can just write her a letter that shares how much she means to you. Just tell her that you're thinking about her and praying for your friendship. I KNOW— write a PRAYER! YES! Write out a prayer and then send it to her. Like in the mail with a stamp and all. Yay!

Sweet Section

4

Fohawks, divorce, homeschooling, parents—and everything family

I really want a fohawk, but my mom is afraid it will make me look like a boy. What should I do? —*Fo-girl*

Cam: I'm a little unsure with this one because I don't even know what a fohawk is. But I guess I can sort of relate because we all run into issues with our parents now and then. I've never wanted a fohawk, but I've wanted other things that my parents didn't agree with or allow me to have.

One of the things I love about the Bible is that there are **Sweet Truths** that apply to lots of different situations. You know, like honoring your parents is always a must, no matter what—even when we don't like what they say, feel that they don't understand us, or even if we really disagree with them. I'll confess I've had my share of "issues" with this at times, but I know my mom and dad have my best interests at heart. They're a gift from God, and they're always looking out for me. And as much as I hate to admit it, they usually see the big picture in a way I can't.

I guess I think that God is more concerned with your heart than your hair. Sometimes it comes down to what's more important: your relationship with your mom or wearing your hair the way you want to. In the end, as disappointing as it might be to let go of the fohawk, it will make your mom feel loved and respected by you, and you'll gain God's approval and be closer to Him—that's worth a lot more.

Erin: For sure this seems like one of those crazy things where the issue really isn't the issue. I mean, it's not really about the haircut as much as your relationship with your mom—and God. Whatever her reasons are, she's your mom and whether it's about a hairstyle, curfew, music, a movie, or whatever...the issue is—are you going to listen and obey her from your heart (as best as you can)? Or...are you going to insist on having it your way?

Another thing I was thinking about is, have you tried to talk to your mom about the way you feel and about the way she feels? I know when my attitude is right, my mom is a lot more likely to listen to me than when I come off like she has no clue what she's talking about—YIKES! I mean, when I respect her, she's more likely to listen to what I have to say.

For example, have you asked her to explain why she's so concerned about the fohawk? Have you *really tried to understand her point of view?* Talking this out with your mom could help to keep your relationship strong, which is really the main thing. I can't help but think of Luke 6:31, "Do to others as you would have them do to you." If you were a mom instead of a daughter, how would you want to be treated? I guess in the end I'd ask, what's the most loving way you can handle this whole thing?

Above all, love each other deeply, because love covers over a multitude of sins. —1 Peter 4:8

Since we're talking about hairstyles, what's your favorite? Do you have curly, naturally wavy (like Cam), or straight hair (like Erin)?

Is your hair long or short?

We think it would be fun to experiment with some cool hairstyles so come on, check it out!

CAM CLIPS CODE: COOL HAIRSTYLES

Sometimes I don't want to do what my mom and dad tell me to do. What can I do about this? —*Peaches*

Cam: Well, I have to kinda laugh, not at you or your question, but because I can so relate! I guess we all have situations where what our parents tell us to do doesn't exactly agree with what we want to do. However, the Bible is pretty clear about what our attitude toward our parents should be. Exodus 20:12 says, "Honor your father and your mother, so that you may live long in the land the Lord your God is giving you." It's one of the Ten Commandments, so obviously it's very important to God. If it's important to God, it should be very important to us.

Erin: It's not always easy to do what our parents say, so don't be too hard on yourself or beat yourself up over this—it's totally normal for someone your age to disagree with your parents. As far as what to do about it, recognize that God put your parents in your life as parents and not peers (another word for someone your age that's a friend). Respect them, and realize that even though they don't seem to understand you all of the time, they do love you and want the best for you. That being said, pray and ask God to give you a right heart toward them, even when you don't agree with them. God is for you and He'll help you.

Just Cool

So we were thinking that sometimes the best way to appreciate what you have—in this case, your parents—is to write down all the reasons why you're thankful for them. So let's do it, girl! Get writing!

MY PARENTS ROCK BECAUSE . . .

I just got home from a week at camp, and I was very homesick. What do you do when you're missing home and your family? Do you have a favorite verse that would help me with this? —Bailes

Cam: It's really hard to be away from home and your family and loved ones. I struggle with this too but in a backward sort of way. My dad often travels for speaking engagements and stuff. Sometimes he's gone for just a couple days but sometimes it can be longer and that's really hard. My mom has to travel sometimes too and when they both have to be gone, that's the worst. So I can relate to really missing your family, and I think it's both good and bad.

When we're apart it makes me think about the things I appreciate about my family, what a blessing they are, and I realize all over again how much they mean to me. That's good stuff because it's really easy to take your family for granted even though they mean the world to you, and being separated helps keep you focused on what a treasure they are.

Erin: I feel the same way; I'm crazy about my parents and miss them terribly when they have to be away. In our case I can usually stay in touch with my mom and dad through text messages and phone calls. I don't know if camp lets you do that or they just go with good old-fashioned snail mail (meaning writing a letter and putting it in the mail). But with my cell phone I can send my mom and dad a text just to let them know I'm thinking of them and miss them.

As far as a Bible verse that might help, well, the **Sweet Truth** we share definitely helps me. As I read that I know that my mom and dad love Jesus and walk in His love—and so do I. So even though we're apart physically and miss each other, I know our hearts are close and we are together in Jesus. Nothing, not even many miles, can separate us from His love or the love we have for each other.

For I am convinced that neither death nor life, neither angels nor demons, neither the present nor the future, nor any powers, neither height nor depth, nor anything else in all creation, will be able to separate us from the love of God that is in Christ Jesus our Lord.
—Romans 8:38–39

My parents don't believe in God, and whenever I talk about Jesus or ask questions about God, they get very mad at me. What should I do? —*Faith Girl*

Cam: For a long time my daddy didn't believe either, so I have some idea of what that can be like. Well, actually, it wasn't like my daddy didn't believe that God existed. He believed in God, but he hadn't given his heart fully to Jesus. He respected our faith but really didn't want to hear about the Lord. I guess he was sort of mad at God for a while because he didn't understand why God allowed my brother to be so sick and suffer a lot. He never got mad at us for our faith, though— that must be really hard.

First of all, you should absolutely pray for your parents. And live in such a way that they will see God in your life. Let His love shine through in everything you do—like listening to your parents and doing what they ask you to do with a joyful heart. It's not easy, but God will help you because He wants your parents to believe even more than you do.

Erin: Absolutely! Believe me, a clean room can preach louder than a Sunday church service. Live out your faith through the good and bad, the ups and downs, the triumphs and tragedies. Someone once said a person with an experience is never at the mercy of a person with an argument—so they have to see and experience God through the way that you live. To put it another way, you can't preach it and speak it because they don't want to hear it right now, but you can preach with your practice. (Oh that was so COOL! Oh yeah!) With patience, prayer, and a strong loving witness Jesus will reach their hearts through you.

And remember, GOD KNOWS and He is at work in all of this right now. Trust Him to work everything out for your good and His glory. This **Sweet Truth** is one of our absolute favorites.

And we know that in all things God works for the good of those who love him, who have been called according to his purpose. —Romans 8:28

Listen, friend, you can never pray enough—especially for the people in your life who don't know and love Jesus. Right now is a great time to pray! Talk to God about all the people in your life who need a relationship with the Lord. Write down every name and pray specifically for each person. Then ask God to show you what else you can pray about for these special people.

Dear God . . .

My parents got a divorce about two years ago. I'm still really sad and angry. How should I handle this so I can stop thinking about it? —*Jesse*

Cam: I'm so sorry to hear about your parents. It must be really horrible and feel totally unfair to you. I don't know what it's like to go through what you have but Jesus can relate and His heart breaks about it too. What happened is not your fault; you're not responsible for your parents' choices. But how you handle it from here is up to you. Don't let hurt turn into bitterness and hatred—forgive both your mom and dad. You don't have to like what happened (no one would) but it will help if you accept it, do your best to love both your parents and pray for them.

Hey, and being sad and angry isn't a bad thing as long as you don't let these emotions take over. You can't let your feelings get the best of you. You need to re-member to take everything to God—including how you feel about all of this.

Erin: I can't imagine how hard it must be to go through something so heartbreaking. God bless you. The Bible says not to let the sun go down on our anger (Ephesians 4:26), and as unrealistic as that might seem, God wouldn't have said it if He didn't offer the grace and strength to let go of the things that are making us mad. So pray for your parents, pray to accept what you can't change, and pray to walk in the love of God.

And as crazy as this may sound—thank God. Yep, I said to thank God. Thank God for everything you're going through right now. He has allowed these circumstances into your life for a purpose that you might not be able to understand right now. Choose to trust Him anyway.

Make your life count for Christ and ask Him to replace that anger with a sense of destiny and meaning. Ask Him what He wants you to both be and do from here. Your mom and dad love you and didn't want you to get caught up in their conflict. Even after two years I'll bet they are still learning how to get over it themselves and could use your prayers and understanding. Let all of the things you're feeling move your heart closer and closer to Jesus.

Sweet Truth Be joyful always; pray continually; give thanks in all circumstances, for this is God's will for you in Christ Jesus.
—1 Thessalonians 5:16

Just Cool

Sometimes you feel like you can't...but GOD CAN! We have a great idea, but you'll have to watch this **Cam Clip** in order to find out. So DON'T MISS OUT—CHECK IT OUT!

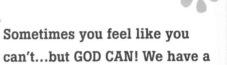

CAM CLIPS CODE: GOD CAN

My mother is trying to quit smoking. How can I help encourage her? —Betsy

Cam: Hey, that's awesome! We all know how unhealthy smoking is and I think it's great that your mother is willing to go for it! I've never smoked (THANK GOD—and I never plan to even try it!), but I have learned that it can be really, really hard to break its power so she'll need a lot of encouragement, understanding, and support. I think you just need to be the best cheerleader you can be. Let her know how proud you are of her for fighting this fight, and be as understanding as you can if it all gets the best of her from time to time.

Erin: Another thing is to be really positive should she cave in and have a cigarette. Let her know it's okay to stumble and fall, but just not to stay down—let your encouragement offer her a loving hand back up again. Nicotine, the substance in cigarettes that causes all the trouble, is a fierce addiction—worse than some illegal drugs. So another thing that might help is to do things with her, things that distract her and get her mind off her cigarette cravings.

Above all, be in prayer. See if there is a prayer chain at your church that you can put your mother on. Stop and pray together as well; it will encourage her and move God to act on her behalf. Keep her inspired; give her a reason to keep fighting. Your mom has to want to do this for herself, but if she sees it means a lot to you too, that's only going to encourage her and help her overcome! I'm so excited for you because this is a really cool opportunity for you to come alongside your mom and get closer to her and deepen your relationship with her. In her weakness, you can help her to be strong!

Sweet Truth **Whatever I have, wherever I am, I can make it through anything in the One who makes me who I am. I don't mean that your help didn't mean a lot to me—it did. It was a beautiful thing that you came alongside me in my troubles.** —Philippians 4:13–14 (*The Message*)

SUPPA SWEET:
Your mom is going to need some extra love and encouragement right now, so let's do something fun. (Oh, and you can do this for anyone in your life who you think might need it.)

Think of one place where you know your mother spends a lot of time—

maybe the laundry room, bathroom, the car. Pick a place. Now get crafty! Make a huge poster out of a bunch of paper or cardboard—make it big enough so it's huge. On your poster board write this—big, bold, and colorful—*God is for you! Nothing is impossible with Jesus! Trust Him with all your heart, and press on with HOPE!*

Now put the poster where you know your mom will see it often during the day.

I lied to my parents, and I don't know what to do. —*Freaking Out*

Cam: Yikes, I'd be freaking out too. The good thing is that you want to bring it out into the light. Keeping a lie tucked away and hidden will only make things worse. Telling your parents everything is absolutely the best thing to do. I would probably write a letter to my parents, explaining everything. It's just easier for me to write everything down because sometimes my words just don't come out the way I want them to. Can you relate?

Erin: Usually, one lie leads to another lie...and then another lie to cover up the previous lies. Lying is never okay! I'm so proud of you for wanting to come clean. You absolutely must deal with this. You have to tell your mom and dad.

Before you do anything, you need to go to God. You see, all sin is against God first and foremost. When we sin, we offend God. Of course, He is always willing to forgive us, but we need to come to Him with a repentant heart.

What does that mean exactly? Well, are you really sorry for what you've done or do you just want to get it out and get over it? If you're not truly sorry for what you've done, you'll probably do it again. It's just the way it usually goes. If you're not sad over this, ask God to help you to be sincerely sorry for what you've done. He'll help you. He wants things to be made right, not just with your parents but also with Him.

When you're done spending time with God, He will prepare you to talk to your parents. Cam's idea about writing a letter is great. But a face-to-face conversa-

tion after you give them the letter would be absolutely necessary. And you know what else I would suggest to you? Pray with your mom and dad when you're done talking it all out. Prayer changes things—especially your heart.

Another cool thing that just hit me is this— we're to live our lives to glorify God, right? Well, obviously, lying doesn't glorify Him but telling the truth and seeking forgiveness does. God is so good that He even allows our mistakes to be turned around for good!

 **And whatever you do, whether in word or deed, do it all in the name of the Lord Jesus, giving thanks to God the Father through him.** —Colossians 3:17

I'm so afraid something is going to happen to my parents. My mom is really sick right now and I'm scared she's going to die. How can I overcome my fears? —*Julianna*

Cam: Well, I totally understand where you're coming from. As you might know, my brother, Hunter, did die because of a disease—so I get what you're saying. My parents (especially my dad) have to travel for speaking engagements, business, and stuff like that (we already talked about this in an earlier devotion). I really hate when they fly because I worry that something will happen to them—like the plane will crash or something. Ugh! I don't even like to think about it or talk about it.

I know I should probably share more, but let's see what Erin has to say.

Erin: Aww, Cam, I'm here for you, and I know how hard it is for you to answer this question. It's hard for me too. First of all, when someone we love is sick, it's scary. It just is. And in a way, I think it's okay to be afraid as long as your fear leads you into the arms of Jesus. He's the only one who fully understands exactly how you feel.

We live in a world full of sin, and that's why evil, sickness, and death occur. There's so much to be afraid of, but God doesn't want us to be fearful. He wants us to come to Him with everything—absolutely everything. He wants us to trust Him with what we don't understand. He wants us to overcome fear with FAITH. Easier said than done, right?

Here's the deal. The more we get to know and love God, the more we trust Him. God loves us more than we can possibly understand. He will not allow anything to come into your life that is not somehow meant for your good and His glory. Trust me, sometimes things will happen that make absolutely no sense—which is why it's so important to know how much God loves us.

Sweet Truth

There is no fear in love. But perfect love drives out fear, because fear has to do with punishment. The one who fears is not made perfect in love. —1 John 4:18

GETTING REAL WITH GOD:

We have a great idea. Let's do this—go get an envelope, a piece of paper, and something to write with. Find a quiet place where you can be alone. Now, get honest and real with God. Talk to Him about everything you're afraid of right now. Write it all down on paper. Please don't rush through this—take as much time as you need. He's listening!

Now, when you're done, seal your envelope. On the front of the envelope write this: *GOD LOVES ME!* Lastly, put your envelope in a safe place (maybe tucked into your Bible).

One more thing! Every time you sense fear trying to overcome you, go and find your envelope—read what you wrote on the front and remember—GOD LOVES YOU! He'll take care of all that concerns you.

I'm homeschooled, so I'm with my family all the time. I feel sort of trapped and sheltered from the real world and wish I could experience and see what life is really like. —*Trapped Girl*

Cam: I don't feel trapped the same way, but I do sort of get what you're saying. I attend a Christian school and feel removed from real life sometimes. There's a lot of reasons parents homeschool their children. Sometimes people homeschool because they think public schools teach things that don't agree with what they believe—for example, prayer is not allowed in public school and some parents might not think this is good. Another reason some families might choose homeschooling is so parents can protect their children from things that they feel aren't good for them.

There are a couple things that I'm thinking right now. First, time is on your side! Um, well, sort of. What I mean is that this school thing only lasts a few years, and then the real world is waiting—it's not going anywhere! I'm not trapped in my home, but I do attend a school that shelters me from a lot of ungodly things—that's not a bad thing. Eventually, you and I will be out in the world making our own decisions and we'll be thankful for all the ways we've been protected. My cousins are homeschooled, and they love it. In fact, I used to beg my mother to homeschool me. Ha! Seriously, I did!

Erin: Maybe you could talk to your parents and work out some sort of way to experience different things. There are true dangers out there in the world, but so many beautiful things too. You know your parents, so maybe if you write up a sort of proposal that respects their values and the reasons they want to homeschool you, yet proposes practical, real ways for you to experience life, they would go for it. What do you have to lose?

Maybe if you start with a sort of mission statement that discusses the beauty of God's creation, your desire to experience it, and why it's reasonable and healthy, then follow up with hands-on ideas, it might just help them understand where you're coming from. I don't think they want to stop you from growing and learning, they just want to give you the best and protect you as much as possible. Maybe this is a real-world way to work with them.

 **Trust in the Lord with all your heart and lean not on your own understanding; in all your ways acknowledge him, and he will make your paths straight.** —Proverbs 3:5–6

All growing up, my sisters told me that I was stupid because I have dyslexia. They've called me ugly because I have dark hair and glasses. Because I grew up with everyone telling me that I'm ugly and stupid, I believe it. I don't feel pretty. How do I stop feeling so down on myself? —*Sarah*

Cam: I'm so sorry that you have had such an unloving experience with those who should love you unconditionally and accept you no matter what. First, let's talk truth: Dyslexia has nothing to do with your intelligence. Some of the most successful people in history have overcome dyslexia. For example, Pablo Picasso is one of the most celebrated painters to ever hold a brush. Steve Jobs, cofounder of Apple (the guy who created the iPod and iPhone—yeah, that guy), is one of the great people of modern technology.

Your family may have put you down and labeled you as ugly and stupid—but that's not what God says about you. Remember, one with God is a majority, and as the Bible says, "What, then, shall we say in response to these things? If God is for us, who can be against us?" (Romans 8:31). And believe me, God is for you… and He's the one to turn to when things like this try to steal your joy.

Erin: It's sad that people who should have made you feel like a superstar have helped to shape your low self-esteem. I'm really sorry. But I have some GREAT NEWS for you! You don't have to listen to those lies—and, yes, they are lies. Don't hang on to them, don't believe them, and don't waste tomorrow's dreams on yesterday's nightmares! (Hey, that was a good one. ☺)

The Bible is very clear that God thinks the world of you, has created you with purpose and potential, and has got some awesome plans for you. If you want a reason to fail there are always plenty of those, and maybe you grew up with them. But my best advice is to forgive your family, stop listening to their lies, and start listening to what God says you are while you begin to follow His call on your life.

Jeremiah 29:11 is one of our favorite Bible verses: "'For I know the plans I have for you,' declares the LORD, 'plans to prosper you and not to harm you, plans to give you hope and a future.'" Unlike your family, the Lord wants to prosper you, give you hope, and build you a future—I doubt that is the destiny or description of someone who's stupid. With Christ we're all winners! Go for it and listen to what Jesus says about you, not those who lie to you and put you down.

Sweet Truth

I can do everything through him who gives me strength. —Philippians 4:13

My dad was drinking and driving and got arrested for it. I still love him, but I'm not sure how to tell him how angry I am about what he did. *—Kelly*

Cam: Wow, this is hard! Maybe you should run it by your mother for a couple reasons: First, it would get it off of your chest and lift a little pressure. Second, she could maybe help you decide whether or not to talk to your father. She must have been pretty upset about the incident, so she can relate and help you decide if it's worth it to say something.

The amazing, cool thing is that the Lord doesn't hold our mistakes over our heads but offers forgiveness. Whatever you decide, remember to let love be your guiding light, and try to put yourself in your father's place— you know, walk a mile in his shoes. I understand your anger and don't blame you at all. However, at this point, try to honestly decide if you have forgiven your father, or if you are holding his mistake against him.

Erin: No one is perfect. In fact, God tells us in His Word that we have all sinned and fallen short of His glory. The amazing thing is that God didn't leave us hopeless and helpless in our sin; He did something about it—HE SENT JESUS! And because of what Jesus did on our behalf we have forgiveness, hope, and everything else we need.

Your dad made a terrible mistake, and he's paying the consequences for his choice. I can't even imagine how bad he must feel.

He can't change what's already been done, right? We can't redo our past. All we can do is look to God and trust Him with our future.

To be honest with you, I'm not so sure you should tell your dad that you're angry with him. I don't think telling him will help him or you. If you need to express to him how you feel about everything, you might want to consider praying about it first. God needs to give you the

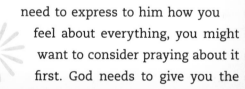

right heart and words in order to share how you're feeling with your dad in a way that would still show respect toward your dad.

 **That God was reconciling the world to himself in Christ, not counting men's sins against them. And he has committed to us the message of reconciliation.**
—2 Corinthians 5:19

Sweet Section

5

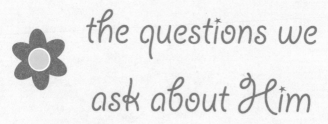

God and

the questions we

ask about Him

How can I learn about God and how can He help me in my everyday life? —*Sophia Lynn*

Cam: I was six years old when I started to learn about God. I asked Him to come into my heart and be my Savior. This was when I started writing my thoughts and prayers in journals. When I started spending time with God and getting closer to Him while I was writing, He helped me, gave me comfort, and I learned more and more about Him.

The Lord has helped me a lot in my everyday life, through ordinary struggles that we all deal with and extraordinary challenges that were really heartbreaking, like the loss of my brother. Nothing I have faced has even come close to that. I will always trust Him. I'm young, so of course I still have so much to learn, but I know that God will help me to know Him more every single day as I walk through life's many experiences. In the fifth chapter of the Book of Romans, it talks about experiences in everyday life making us stronger, shaping our character, and building our hope. So there's a reason for the things we go through: They teach us about God, how to trust Him, and how to hope in Him (that's in

Romans 5:4–5). He wants you to know Him more and uses our experiences, good and bad, to help us do just that! Just talk to Him about this and everything! He's awesome!

Erin: I would start with prayer. Ask God to reveal Himself to you just like He promises to in Jeremiah 33:3 when He says, "Call to me and I will answer you and tell you great and unsearchable things you do not know." God has already showed us what He's like in three very specific ways. First of all, just look around. God has displayed who He is through creation. All the amazing things God has made show us how extraordinary He is. He has also revealed Himself to us through His Word—the Bible. You will find everything you need to know about God and His plan for your life in the Bible. It's awesome; you should absolutely check it out. Lastly, you can learn about God through Jesus, His Son. We learn about the life of God's Son through reading His story in the Bible, and we can have a personal relationship with Him through His Spirit, which dwells in our heart.

I started learning about God at a very young age. When I was just five years old, I asked Jesus to come into my life. I'll never forget that day for as long as I live. By setting an example and giving me a solid faith foundation at a very young age, my parents have also helped me to grow and continue to mature in my relationship with the Lord.

God wants to be involved in every part of your life. Get to know Him! Ask Him to guide you every day as you grow in your faith.

When you call on me, when you come and pray to me, I'll listen. When you come looking for me, you'll find me.
—Jeremiah 29:12–13 (*The Message*)

Let's talk to some people and find out how they learn more about God and how He has helped them in their everyday lives.

 **CAM CLIPS** CODE: EVERYDAY LIFE

Why does it feel as if God doesn't talk to us? How do we know He is talking to us? —*BK*

Cam: This is a great question that I think everyone has asked at least once. We know God talks to us through His Word, the Bible, and He speaks to our hearts by His Spirit. But if you're like me, maybe you've wondered why we can't actually hear Him or see Him even though we know He's here with us—why doesn't He show Himself or speak out loud? And how can we really know His voice in our hearts or what direction He wants us to go in our lives? When we get to heaven we will see Him face to face. How amazing is that? Until then He helps us to know who He is through His Word—which someone once described as a "love letter." So read it girl. ☺

Erin: Like Cam said, I think a lot of people have asked this question at some point in their walk with the Lord (myself included). God talks to us through His Word—the Bible—and through His Son, Jesus. The more we read His Word, the more we'll know and love God.

I'm sure He uses circumstances to speak to us and guide us too—but for me, it all comes back to the Bible. Circumstances can be confusing to figure out and that rumbling within us can be the pizza we had for dinner (hmm, not so sure about that comparison), but the Bible is His Word—period.

We don't read the Bible just to know things about God; we read it to really **KNOW** Him—to know who He is and what He's like, and to understand His character. Getting to know God is the greatest gift we've been given, and He is really unknowable unless He reveals Himself to us. And He has. He's not playing hide-and-seek with us; He wants us to know Him. Even when we don't feel like God is talking to us, He's still there working everything out for good in the midst of our lives. Oh, and we know He's talking to us because He said He is. Check out the **Sweet Truth**. Oh, and I was just thinking, it's really not about how we "feel," in other words, we don't have to feel as if God is talking to us because it's not about feelings—it's about the truth—no matter how we feel. That was the longest run-on sentence in history. Sorry!

Sweet Truth

In the past God spoke to our forefathers through the prophets at many times and in various ways, but in these last days he has spoken to us by his Son, whom he appointed heir of all things, and through whom he made the universe. The Son is the radiance of God's glory and the exact representation of his being, sustaining all things by his powerful word. —Hebrews 1:1–3

How can I get closer to God when I doubt Him? I'm a Christian but don't always "feel" like one. —*Amelia*

Cam: Hmm, well the only way I know how to get closer to God is to spend time with Him. Read the Bible. Write in your prayer journal. Pray. I also think the enemy tries to tempt us to think that because we don't *feel* close to God that we might not be a real Christian. He is a liar. He wants us to doubt Jesus and His love for us. It's ridiculous. I remember a time when the enemy tempted me to doubt, and it was horrible. But I got through it with

156

prayer, reading verses, my parents and other Christians praying for me, and trusting God.

GOD loves you!

His love doesn't change. Whether we feel like our faith is strong or weak, His love is always there! He wants to be close to you! Talk to Him about this and trust that He will help you to draw near to Him.

One way to look at it is that no matter what we feel, we walk with God through faith, not feelings. Hebrews 11:6 says, "And without faith it is impossible to please God, because anyone who comes to him must believe that he exists and that he rewards those who earnestly seek him." Those times we don't "feel" God, or "doubt" Him, are times we have to walk by faith and believe that He'll keep His promises to us.

Now that's a great reason to memorize Bible verses—so we can hang on to those promises when we struggle against doubt. Faith is sort of like a muscle that gets stronger when we use it. And if you've ever played sports or worked out (something my family is big on with my dad being a football player and all), then you know it's not easy to get stronger—it's hard work. Faith is the same way, and it's the only way I know to overcome doubt. I don't feel stronger after a hard basketball practice. I'm beat—I feel weaker. But the truth is I'm getting stronger because of that workout even though it left me exhausted (and hungry— yep, always thinking about food). Faith is the same way—it grows stronger as we work it out and overcome our doubts. Feelings follow faith, not the other way around.

Erin: What a great question, and a very cool answer from Cam! Love the workout example—since I'm all about keeping my body (or as God would call it—my "temple") in good shape by eating healthy and exercising. Being a Christian isn't easy. We all face trials of many kinds. Some of our trials include moments when we doubt God or question Him—like why does He allow bad things to happen to us if He loves us and stuff like that.

I don't "feel" like I'm a Christian when I'm doubting or not trusting God for whatever reason. We will all doubt God at some point in our walk with Him; it's a natural part of our growth. The devil (our enemy) tempts us to doubt God and question His love for us. I think one of his evil ways is to make us think that we can't get closer to God—that God is far from us. This is a lie! God is always with us and will never leave us.

Being a Christian is not about how we feel. In other words, just because you don't feel like a Christian doesn't mean that you're not one. And just because you don't feel like you're in God's arms doesn't mean He's not holding you close—He is. It's not about our feelings—it's about Jesus and what He did for us. Our feelings can't change what's true. Besides, our feelings change all the time. Jesus is always the same; HE doesn't change so His love is always there for us no matter what. It was there before we believed in it and it's there whether we feel it or not.

THIS IS A **HUGE** RELIEF TO ME!

If you have received forgiveness through Jesus then you are HIS, and nothing will ever change this! Not your feelings, not what others say, not what you do or say...NOTHING! Oh, and to answer the question (LOL), I get closer to God through reading His Word and spending time with HIM! He helps me to be closer to Him as I spend time with Him.

Does God have a purpose for my life, even though I'm young? —*e.m.k.*

Cam: Absolutely! Destiny is a HUGE thing. (And it's a cool girl's name! Ha!) But the fact is, there are things no one but you can do, because God made you—YOU. You were born when you were, where you were, to the family you were born into for reasons far greater than we could ever understand.

The Bible has a number of young ones who influenced their worlds for various reasons, people like Samuel, David, Joseph, and others who made differences, small and large, at very young ages. That's one of the things I love about knowing the Lord. I know my life matters even at a young age. I know that what I do as I live for him as a SWEET *HCWG* girl (SWAG!—just had to add that) will influence eternity and make a difference in the lives of others!

Listen, if you were standing in front of me right now (I wish you were) I would grab hold of your arms, look into your eyes, and tell you with as much excitement as I can express—GOD CREATED YOU, GIRL—for a purpose. Right now, He is doing a work in your life...and it's good—suppa good!

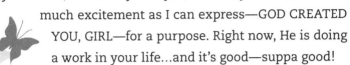

Erin: I believe with all my heart that God has a purpose and perfect plan for your life. Though you are young and may not know what it is yet, God knows. There are times when I try to figure out what God's plan is for me. But then I'm reminded that His plan is always greater than my own and I need to let Him prepare me and mold me into the person He wants me to be so I can fulfill His plan.

We were all created with a purpose. God may have you in a place you never thought you would find yourself. Even though you are young put your faith in Him because He knows the outcome and whatever it is it will be AMAZING because it's HIS plan for you.

Ultimately, we were made to glorify God and we do that by loving Him and honoring Him through our obedience to His Word. Sometimes that word "obedience" makes us squirm because we think of rules and how we often break them, right? Well, hear this, my friend—the more you LOVE God, the more you will long to follow after His heart and Word. So...let's do this—let's ask God to help us to LOVE HIM MORE. Okay! You'll find journal space below, and I'll get us going in prayer.

 **Sweet Truth** — **Don't let anyone look down on you because you are young, but set an example for the believers in speech, in life, in love, in faith and in purity.** —1 Timothy 4:12

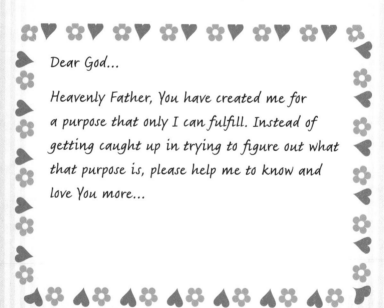

Dear God...

Heavenly Father, You have created me for a purpose that only I can fulfill. Instead of getting caught up in trying to figure out what that purpose is, please help me to know and love You more...

The Bible is so old, so how can it help us today? —*Bailey*

Cam: I'm laughing right now because I used to think the very same thing. Of course I thought the Bible was old because, come on, people in the Old Testament lived to be like eight hundred years old and stuff. And what about that lady Sarah, Abraham's wife? She had her first child when she was ninety years old or something. That's unbelievable. And that's one of the reasons I love the Bible so much—because God is not like us. He is God and does what only God can do.

The cool thing is that we only know what we know until we learn and know more. Basically, the more you get to know and understand God, the more you realize how very much the Bible speaks to us right now, today. It's actually quite amazing. But then again, if God wrote it, it's more than amazing; it's out of this world.

Erin: Although the Bible was written a long time ago, God wrote it in such a way that it can still be applied to our lives today. Isn't that amazing? Even way back then God was thinking about us. In fact, before time even began, God was thinking about us. The more you read God's Word, the more you'll learn how it can be applied to your everyday life. We can learn so much about God and ourselves by reading and meditating on what God did and how He led His people. Now, when I say "meditating," I don't mean some weirdness like humming and sitting on the floor or something. Meditating is taking the time to stop and think and pray about what you're reading.

The Bible is always fresh and new. You could read it a million times and still find that God is teaching you something new. Same with *Hot Chocolate With God*! Read it a million times and you will still laugh your head off...okay, just kidding!

One more very important thing to remember: We read the Bible to know God. Not just know about Him—but to really know and love Him. It's not like any other book ever written; it's living, it's true, and it speaks to our hearts. It's not just paper, ink, and glue—words and ideas on pages stuck between two covers. Everything God wants us to know about Him is found in His Word. So get reading, girl!

Sweet Truth

The grass withers and the flowers fall, but the word of our God stands forever.
—Isaiah 40:8

Just Cool

Okay, maybe you're not familiar with the Bible and need a bit of guidance—a little help to get you started. Well, fear not, the Kelly girls are here for you. Come with us and we'll show you how we do everything Bible...um and more. Ha-ha-ha—you'll have to watch to find out!

CAM CLIPS CODE: BIBLE BASICS

Why doesn't God heal everybody, all the time? —*Kiley*

Cam: WOW, talk about a hard question. Yikes!

If you're familiar with the other books in the HCWG series, you know that my older brother, Hunter, went to heaven when he was just eight and a half years old. I was six when it happened. Hunter had a terrible disease that even to this day I don't really understand.

I don't remember everything about what happened while my brother was alive, but I do remember that we prayed—in fact we prayed a lot (like all the time)—especially for Hunter to be healed. But Hunter wasn't healed here on earth.

Even though I prayed and hoped that God would rescue Hunter from this disease, He didn't. I wish I knew why. But the truth is, even if God told me why, knowing why wouldn't take away my heartbreak. I miss my brother every minute of every day.

I thank God that my brother is healed now. He's in heaven, and someday I will see him again. I can't wait.

Erin: What a great question. I'm not sure Cam and I can adequately answer this question, but you asked and we think you deserve to know how we feel about it.

I don't know why God doesn't heal everyone, every time. I don't know why He chose not to heal my brother. I don't understand why He allows some people to survive cancer and others to die from it. I just don't know. But I do know and believe that God is good all the time. He sees the bigger picture, the future, and He knows exactly how everything is going to turn out.

As my mom always says, "This is not the end of the story."

Death is not the end. Life here on earth is not the end. Heaven and eternity await us. We have so much to look forward to.

God's ways are sometimes beyond our ability to understand. So I guess we have a choice—will we trust God to heal and will we trust Him when He doesn't?

There's no easy way to answer this question, but I do think this **Sweet Truth** helps put everything in perspective.

"For my thoughts are not your thoughts, neither are your ways my ways," declares the LORD. "As the heavens are higher than the earth, so are my ways higher than your ways and my thoughts than your thoughts."
—Isaiah 55:8–9

🖊️ ✦ **Journal It** Write down all the people in your life who need healing right now. Be specific. After you've written down the names, talk to God about all of these people by name.

How can we share God with a person who doesn't believe or doesn't want to listen? —*LC012*

Cam: It's so sad that some people don't want to listen to anything you have to say about God. If these people are in your family it's even worse because they're family and of course you want them to know God.

We can't force people to listen or believe. But we can pray! Pray and pray and keep on praying until God opens the door to the unbeliever's heart. While you wait and pray, ask God to prepare you to share the good news about Jesus. Ask Him to make you ready to give a reason for the great hope that you have in your heart. People want to know how God has changed your heart and life. Sharing your story of how you came to know Jesus is a huge privilege. If you love the Lord and understand that everyone on the face of the earth needs Him, you'll want to share your hope in Him with everyone. You'll want people to know how much God loves them.

Erin: The truth is, unfortunately, there are some people who just don't want to listen and don't want to hear what you have to say about God. What's really cool is you don't always have to tell them, you can show them. People who don't know God are watching the people who do—especially during difficult circumstances.

When you live your life for Christ you're set apart and different from the rest of the world. People will see the way you act and how you treat others and they'll notice that something is different about you.

Although it's very important and part of God's mission for us to tell people about Jesus, sometimes it's more effective to show them Jesus—who He is and how He is working through your life.

Sweet Truth **Be imitators of God, therefore, as dearly loved children and live a life of love, just as Christ loved us and gave himself up for us as a fragrant offering and sacrifice to God.** —Ephesians 5:1–2

Pray also for me, that whenever I open my mouth, words may be given me so that I will

fearlessly make known the mystery of the gospel for which I am an ambassador in chains. Pray that I may declare it fearlessly, as I should.
—Ephesians 6:19–20

How do we stay focused on God when there are so many distractions all around us? —*Jessica*

Cam: Sometimes I feel like I'm the queen of distractions. Girlfriend, I get off on tangents and get distracted all the time. Seriously, my mom will tell me to do something and I'll go to do it and then end up doing something totally different. UGH! I know this example is sort of different than what the question is referring to—but I got distracted. HA-HA-HA!

No really, in order to stay more focused on God we need to pay attention to how we're spending our time. God cares about what we put into our minds and hearts. He wants to spend time with us and cares about how we choose to spend our time. We only have a certain number of hours in a day. If we focus our time on the things that are mentioned in the **Sweet Truth**, we'll draw closer and closer to God. The cool thing is that when we get closer to Him we want less and less of the distractions of this world.

Erin: I'm a work in progress, and so are you. We all have so much to learn, and God isn't finished with us yet. He knows that the world is full of distractions. Every day His mercy is new for each and every one of us. I'm so thankful that God is so merciful and gracious because I don't always get it right every time. Sometimes I'm completely focused on my walk with the Lord, and other times I let other meaningless things get in the way.

I think one of the best ways to stay focused on God would be to spend more time with Him. The more we get to know God, the more we want to know Him. The more we know Him, the more we love Him. The more we love Him, the more we want to live for Him and please Him. It all starts with Him.

If we really want to please the Lord, we will make the effort to eliminate the many distractions in our lives. Trust me, this isn't easy, but we can pray and trust God to help us one day at a time.

Sweet Truth

Finally brothers, whatever is true, whatever is noble, whatever is right, whatever is pure, whatever is lovely, whatever is admirable, if anything is excellent or praiseworthy, think about such things. —Philippians 4:8

It's sometimes hard to know what to pray and how to pray because there's so much to be praying about and so many people that need prayer. —*lucy*

Cam: Oh, girl, I totally agree. It seems like everybody has something going on that they need prayer for. How can we even keep track of it all? At school we have a time in the morning and in Bible class when everyone has an opportunity to share a prayer request. After everyone shares what's on his or her heart, we pray. I love this because I would never know that people in my class need prayer for specific things if we didn't talk about it.

I think journaling is a great way to remember what you need to be praying about. A prayer journal is also cool because you can look back and see all the ways in which God answered your prayers.

Erin: What's really comforting and amazing to me is the fact that God says He knows the words that will come forth from our mouths before we even utter them. He already knows what we're going to say before we say it—so He already knows who needs prayer before we do. I love what the **Sweet Truth** says. When we're struggling to find the right words to pray the Spirit sort of takes over for us. He prays for us. WOW! The Holy Spirit intercedes (which is another word for prays) for us when we just can't seem to find the words. I have to say it again—WOW.

One more thing. Mommy has said before that our tears are like prayers too. Sometimes tears just flow when words don't. And that's okay because God already knows, and in our weakness He is strong!

Sweet Truth

In the same way, the Spirit helps us in our weakness. We do not know what we ought to pray for, but the Spirit himself intercedes for us with groans that words cannot express. —Romans 8:26

Just Cool

My mom has what she calls a Prayer Board in her office where she puts up everything she wants to remember to pray about. Ya know what? Instead

of trying to explain this to you, I'll just show you. Come on, let's go.

CAM CLIPS CODE: PRAYER BOARD

So here is your very own Prayer Board. Use your imagination and make it look really cool. And don't forget to PRAY!

PRAYER BOARD

What would you do if someone said, "God is stupid and you're a weirdo?" —*the squirrely one*

Cam: Clearly the person saying this doesn't know God at all. If he or she did, they wouldn't talk like this about God, or you for that matter. Can you even imagine how God must feel when people say horrible things about Him? It makes me feel so sad just thinking about it. I would want to say something back to this person, but it would probably only make matters worse.

Your best response is to walk away and pray. Hey, that's good—WALK AWAY AND PRAY! We need to write that one down for sure...and do it. I bet we could even come up with a cool rap song to help us remember what to do the next time something like this happens. Yeah, sorry if I'm getting carried away.

Let's see what Erin thinks about this.

Erin: My initial response to this would probably be to start defending God. But here's the thing, God doesn't need me to defend Him. He's completely capable of taking care of Himself in every way.

God is also your defender. He hears what people say

to you. He knows when mean words hurt you. He cares about every single detail of your life. When things like this happen we need to remember that God is in the midst of the situation.

We can't control what other people do and say, but we can control how we respond. Like Cam said, this person obviously doesn't know God. When someone says stuff against God or His children, it doesn't go unnoticed. God sees, and He will take care of it in His perfect timing.

As hard as it is sometimes to be kind to people like this, that really should be our response. Just think about it—this person is lost and doesn't know God. They have no idea that what they're saying is really bad because they don't know Him. If you pray for this person, maybe God will open his or her heart to hear the truth. Pray for wisdom so you can respond in love.

Oh, and Cam? I love the rap song idea. Do it!

Sweet Truth

Be wise in the way you act toward outsiders; make the most of every opportunity. Let your conversation be always full of grace, seasoned with salt, so that you may know how to answer everyone. —Colossians 4:5-6

TALK IT OUT: I think we need to pray. Talk to God about the people in your life that need to come to know Him.

How do I know for sure if I'm God's child; if I'm saved or not? —*Lamb*

Cam: That's an AWESOME question, and I'm glad you asked. In fact, this is seriously the most important question any of us can ever ask. A lot of people ask that question because they don't *feel* saved, or *feel* like a child of God, so they worry and wonder and want some evidence to make them feel that it's a done deal!

Well, like I said that's an awesome question, and awesome questions often have awesome answers! Just so you know up front, there have been a lot of books written about this, so to give you something to take away in a couple paragraphs is going to be like really hard! But here goes...

First, it's all about the Bible! It starts and ends there—you must believe that the Scriptures are in fact the actual Word of God; like a "love letter" from heaven to our hearts! I love thinking of God's Word as a "love letter" because it seriously helps me to want to read it more. Just being honest here.

The Bible tells us everything we need to know! It's all in the BOOK!

Listen, fairy tales don't change lives! God does!

I know a lot of lives that have been changed, really changed by the love of God and by the Word of God. Look at it this way: The more you live according to the Word of God, the more like the Word of God you become—now you've got to admit that's way cool! I've seen people who have gone from being empty and sad to being alive and filled with hope and joy. They didn't read a self-help book or drink some magic blue Kool-Aid; JESUS changed them!

So basically, what I'm trying to say is that you know that you're God's child if your life has been changed; if you live for Him instead of yourself.

Erin: It's really not an issue of feeling like His child as much as being His child. If you have done what the Bible describes as necessary to be born again into His family, then you *are* God's child. Think about it, if you've been born again—born from above (John 3:3)—you're His! If you've believed by His grace and been saved apart from any works, then you're saved. If you've become a new creation then all things are new, and you belong to God. I could keep going, but I think you get the idea.

And one last thing—The very fact that you care about whether or not you are saved reflects the Spirit of God already in you. If you didn't believe, I don't think you'd even be asking this question.

Sweet Truth

That if you confess with your mouth, "Jesus is Lord," and believe in your heart that God raised him from the dead, you will be saved. For it is with your heart that you believe and are justified, and it is with your mouth that you confess and are saved. —Romans 10:9-10

HIS LOVE LETTER TO ME: Please look up the following verses and write them down. Then share how you think these apply to you and your life. *LOVE ROCKS!!!*

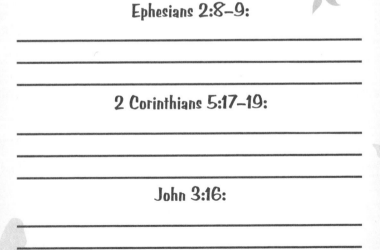

Ephesians 2:8–9:

_____

_____

_____

2 Corinthians 5:17–19:

_____

_____

_____

John 3:16:

_____

_____

_____

Will I become an angel when I get to heaven?
—*Stephanie*

Cam: Let me just say this, how cool would it be to have wings like the angels do in all the pictures? Please tell me I'm not the only girl in the world who has dreamed about being able to fly. Okay, back to your question. The way I read the Bible, which is really where we get the only true information about what comes next, angels are angels and people are people—we're different.

There are not a lot of verses (I asked my mother ☺) about who and what angels are or what they do, but there is enough in the Scriptures to make it very clear that they are different from people. For example, when Jesus returns, He's going to send angels to gather believers from throughout the earth (Mark 13:27). And in 1 Corinthians 6:3, the Bible says that we will judge the angels—how cool is *that*!

So no, you won't become an angel once you get to heaven; you'll be changed, but you'll still be you! I know my time will come, but I seriously can't wait to get to heaven. Now that's SWEET!

Erin: I think this idea that people become angels when they get to heaven came from Matthew 22:30, "At the resurrection people will neither marry nor be given in marriage; they will be like the angels in heaven." The thing is, the Lord wasn't saying we'd sprout wings, grow a halo, and be miraculously turned into angels—ha-ha-ha. He was explaining that our lives will be completely different once this life has passed—and the example He used was marriage, meaning people will not be married in heaven. (So start praying for a godly husband now—ha-ha-ha! Just kid-ding—but not really!)

Even though things change a lot be-tween time and eternity, we will always be who God created us to be, and that's comforting to me. Angels are really cool and power-ful spiritual beings, but they will never be people. People are awesome beings created in God's very image and will never be angels.

God didn't put angels in charge of this business of salvation that we're dealing with here. It says in Scripture, What is man and woman that you bother with them; why take a second look their

way? You made them not quite as high as angels, bright with Eden's dawn light; Then you put them in charge of your entire handcrafted world.
—Hebrews 2:5–8 (*The Message*)

Sort Of Cool or Just Odd: Okay, whatever; I think it would be fun to think up some names for angels. Let's pretend God told us to name His heavenly beings—yeah, I know, but let's have fun with this anyway. Be creative and heavenly! What names would you give to four angels?

1.

2.

3.

4.

Now, use your wild imagination and describe what you think these angels look like. Try to be as detailed as possible.

Will I see my pets in heaven? —*beth ann*

Cam: I can't think of one person who has ever had a pet that he or she cared about who didn't want them to be with them forever. And with God not only being a God of love, but actually being love (1 John 4:8), I've got to believe that the pets that mean so much to us here will be with us someday in heaven!

The Bible says that during Christ's thousand-year rule on the earth (which I don't fully understand, because like I'm young and still learning about Jesus every single day), "The wolf will live with the lamb, the leopard will lie down with the goat, the calf and the lion and the yearling together; and a little child will lead them" (Isaiah 11:3). So we do know that there will be animals during that time, and they won't be wild animals any longer. You've got all these creatures that once were natural enemies, and a little child right there with them, leading them.

The way I see it, everything, and I mean absolutely everything, that we need will be in heaven. And we just don't know for sure if our pets will be there, but I'm hopeful that they will be.

Erin: I think so, and I sure hope so! God made animals, so I believe they will be in heaven with us. God talks about how one day the lion will lay down next to the lamb (like Cam shared). I think this is God showing us that one day there will be animals in heaven, and it will be perfect. And whatever way this will unfold, there is a level of communication between an innocent child and these creatures because a child will lead them. For that to happen, the animals will need to understand the child. There is no way a child is going to lead a wolf or leopard with the way things are now on earth. Plus, God created animals before time existed, so it kind of makes sense that there will be animals once time doesn't exist anymore.

Though the Bible is pretty much silent about pets in heaven, everything I know about God is consistent with the beautiful creatures we loved in this world sharing that love with us in the next.

God made the wild animals according to their kinds, the livestock according to their kinds, and all the creatures that move along the ground according to their kinds. And God saw that it was good. —Genesis 1:25

SUPPA SWEET AND TOTALLY COOL: It's been a while since Erin and I have made a video with our three dogs—yes, we have three dogs—two Labrador Retrievers and one Chihuahua. Since we're talking about pets, we'd love to show you how funny our dogs are, so let's go.

CAM CLIPS CODE: KELLY PETS

Tell us about your pets! Do you have a dog or cat? Maybe a hamster, gerbil, or pet tarantula? Did I just say that? Just typing that word gives me the creepy-crawlies—eww. We can't stand spiders. Eww, so gross! If you don't have a pet, talk about the kind of pet you hope to have someday.

☆

MY
AMAZING
♡ PET ♡

Jovi (dog) Chico (dog)
Jazmin (dog) Izzy (cat)